The Best-Laid Business Plans

How to Write Them,
How To Pitch Them

Paul Barrow

5 7 9 11 10 8 6

First published in Great Britain in 2001 by
Virgin Books
Random House
20 Vauxhall Bridge Road
London
SW1V 2SA

www.virginbooks.co.uk

A catalogue record for this book is available from the British Library.

ISBN 978 0 7535 0963 0

Series Consultant: Professor David Storey
Joint Series Editors: Robert Craven, Grier Palmer

The Random House Group Limited supports The Forest Stewardship
Council® (FSC®), the leading international forest-certification organisation.
Our books carrying the FSC label are printed on FSC®-certified paper.
FSC is the only forest-certification scheme supported by the leading
environmental organisations, including Greenpeace. Our
paper procurement policy can be found at
www.randomhouse.co.uk/environment

Series design by Janice Mather at Ben Cracknell Studios
Typeset by Phoenix Photosetting, Chatham, Kent
Printed and bound in Great Britain by Clays Ltd, St Ives plc

Contents

Foreword
by Sir Richard Branson

It feels a bit odd to be writing a foreword to a business book. Perhaps it's because I haven't always done business by the book myself. Sometimes I've regretted that, and sometimes I've been glad that I followed my instincts instead of doing what conventional advisers might have recommended.

One thing I've learned is that there's no right way to do things in life. There is no 'magic bullet' for success in business. What works for Virgin Atlantic might not be right for British Airways; what suits your business could be completely wrong for someone else's. But any advice that can help you beat the odds and succeed in business has got to be a good thing. Listening to lots of people's ideas before taking a decision has always been something I have strongly believed in.

Every book in this series has been written by an expert in his or her field, and they've come up with lots of interesting and thought-provoking ideas. But the most important thing is to do what you personally feel is right.

Business should be fun. Enjoy what you do, and success comes within reach.

Good luck!

According to the Concise Oxford Dictionary, a plan is 'a detailed proposal for doing or achieving something'.

The first task of this book by Paul Barrow is to convince the reader that a business plan is important for a small business. This is easy when the business is seeking finance from a bank or a venture capitalist since they always require a written document before even considering releasing funds. But this book makes the case that ALL businesses should plan and use the plan for setting objectives. They can then use it for monitoring the achievement of those objectives, and possibly re-setting them.

The clinching argument for planning is that it forces the owner to think first and then act. In any organisation, large or small, individual decisions are often taken 'on the hoof'. Where there are no clearly recognised/understood/written-down objectives for the business, this risks, at best, the business drifting aimlessly. At worst, it leads to internal strife and dissatisfaction, which inevitably communicates itself to customers with disastrous results.

But, if you are not persuaded by such arguments, then the chances are that you would not be even looking at this book in the first place! So, given that you can at least be talked into considering producing a written plan, what gems are in this book?

To me, the key message is that a successful plan has to get both the big and the small picture right. So, what is in the big picture?

First, who is the plan for? Is it for the bank, the venture capitalist, the landlord, a customer, or for internal purposes only? Who, specifically, is going to read it? What do they know about the business – or even the sector? All these influence the nature of the document. In short, this is the fundamental business question – Who is the customer for this document?

The second key question relates to the vexed issue of business – and personal – objectives. These have to be clearly thought out, but also clearly stated. Paul Barrow uses the SMART concept to deal with objectives. He usefully says that objectives must be Specific, Measurable, Achievable, Realistic and Timed. If most small firms – and many other types of organisations – only achieved this goal, this alone would be a huge advance.

Finally, for existing businesses, it is necessary to assess current performance before deciding whether and how to move forward. Paul Barrow provides a swift health check, but those wanting more will find that provided by Robert Craven's book in the Virgin Business Guides series, *Kick-Start Your Business*.

The Best-Laid Business Plans is for people who actually are going to have to write such a plan, possibly for the first time. It has to be the best possible plan, in every detail, if it is achieve its objective of obtaining funding or customers. This means the small – as well as the big – picture also has to be right; it has to look and read as if it has been lovingly crafted. So, what advice does Paul Barrow provide here?

The market has to be researched and documented. The banker/financier has to be convinced the business owner knows who their customers and potential customers are. They need to know who else is in this marketplace and why they should buy the product/ service from one firm rather than another. Sometimes the 'back of an envelope' market calculation is the best available, but my personal opinion is that if there is one key to success which stands out above all others it is understanding customers. Even if financiers don't always place it at the top of the list, this demonstrable understanding has to underpin the plan. This understanding is rarely found on the backs of envelopes.

But the 'little picture' also needs real attention to detail. To some, Paul Barrow's even mentioning of the way the business plan should be presented may border on the insulting. He tells you to use short sentences, to write in plain English, to use wide margins, to bind the appendices separately, to use the spell checker and even to use Times Roman 10-point. But presentation is so important for first impressions. It does not imply that these impressions are always right, but why get off to a bad start when you can get off to a flyer? This book helps you to do just that.

Professor David Storey
Director, Centre for Small and Medium Sized Enterprises
Warwick Business School, University of Warwick

Introduction

One of the biggest problems with most people is their natural enthusiasm to get stuck in. You can imagine the situation: you are doing some DIY, and there in a flat pack on the floor is a mess of wood and screws just waiting to be converted into a work of art. Chances are, if you are anything like me, you rip open the box, give the instructions a cursory glance and, relying on natural ability, start the assembly process. You go straight to the biggest bits. Yes, these look like a top, back and sides. Quickly, using the most obvious fixings, you assemble these. Next, you notice there is a drawer – but ignore this because it can wait. On with the doors, congratulating yourself on how quickly it all seems to be coming together.

At this point you start to question why there are so many smallish bits left over without an obvious use. Also, there are loads of little wooden rods about an inch long with some glue, which you have not used and you are wondering what these are for. A few minutes later you realise that a vital bit is missing and that because you have already put the sides on you cannot fit the runners for the drawer at the top of the unit. You walk away from the unit cursing and saying to yourself, 'How do they expect me to put that together? The instructions were rubbish!'

The moral of the story is painfully obvious. A little bit of reflection and looking at the instructions would have revealed what everything was for (and the fact that a piece was missing), what was needed to fix each piece on and what order things needed to be assembled. In my simple way I would have called this planning and the end result would have been a kitchen unit that you would have been proud of – looking as if it had been built by a master craftsman.

Your business, too, deserves the best possible approach to its planning if it is to be the success that you have in mind. Regardless of whether it is a new business or an existing growing business, you will improve its chances of success if you think first and act later. You need to ask yourself these questions:

- What do you want to achieve?
- How do you want to achieve it?
- What are you going to need to do it?
- What are the critical areas that you need to be aware of to avoid failing?
- How will you know when you have done it?

Managing a business is usually complicated – far more so than assembling a flat-pack kitchen unit. If it is your own business and you get it seriously wrong then at best you lose your livelihood and at worst you lose your home and your savings as well. If you are managing someone else's business – say a publicly quoted company – and you get it wrong at best you don't get promoted and at worst you lose your career. Additionally a lot of shareholders might lose their shirts.

This book is all about improving your chances of success for your business by improving your business planning – both the process (the way you do it) and the resulting document (the business plan). Everything you will read in this book is common sense, easy to use and has worked for lots of other people. No prior knowledge of business planning is required. However if you follow this book you will have subjected your business idea to a most critical review – asked all the searching questions and hopefully found all the answers. Your business plan will then be ready for its next critical audience – the bank manager, your boss, your partner … whoever. After you have got their support, then you can get on with it.

How to use this book

If you follow this book you will have covered everything you need to produce the best possible plan for your business. It will challenge you to think in real depth about your business. If you are superficial and do not ask and get answers to the really tough questions then your business proposition is probably not strong enough to withstand a more critical external scrutiny.

Unfortunately a poorly prepared and presented business plan has a threefold effect:

- You will fail in your initial objective – getting the money you need from the bank/parents/board of directors, etc.
- You have probably queered your pitch even if you go back later with a better business plan – they may be influenced by their negative views of your earlier effort.
- Finally, if timing is critical, the delay while you rewrite and present your business plan may mean you have missed the boat and the opportunity has passed by.

The obvious conclusion must be that on the big day the plan that you present must be the best possible – the tried and tested version, not the first draft. You may get only one shot at it – give it your very best.

While this book is complete in itself – in that it will help you to produce your business plan – it is not a textbook on production, marketing, finance, company/employment law, etc. Chapters of the book will make reference to each of these areas but only in sufficient detail for your business plan. If, however, you feel uncertain about any of these areas then you should seek specialist help. For example you may have some technical or legal questions about employing staff – about what should be contained in a contract of employment and when must an employee receive one. You will find in the appendices further useful reference materials and contacts to help you.

At various stages you will need to find out things that are not technical or legal but are important in completing your business plan. For example, you will certainly need to find out more about your competitors and marketplace. This may include trying to find out who they are, where they are and how financially strong they may be. The appendices will again give you useful pointers as to where you can get this information and more besides.

As you read the book you will see some logic to the order and layout to each of the chapters. In summary the book will cover:

- Why you need a business plan, the benefits and the different audiences for it
- What goes into a winning business plan
- Assessing the current situation
- Business and personal objectives, today, tomorrow, in five years' time
- Financial forecasts – profit, cash flow, balance sheet, funding required
- Customers, competitors and sales forecasts
- Your products or service – an honest assessment
- What resources will you need? – thinking ahead
- Are people part of your plan? – getting it right
- Information gathering to support your business plan
- Contingency plans for when it does not quite go right
- Fine-tuning your business plan to ensure success – revisiting the words and numbers
- Business plan checklist – to make sure you have covered everything
- Useful contacts and sources of information and help
- Turning your plan into reality – delivering the goods
- Your next business plan

Each chapter is liberally supported by real-life examples and some useful tips. Whether you are writing your first business plan or you are a seasoned campaigner you will find that this book is for you. It makes no assumptions about your background – it is equally usable regardless of your area of expertise, be it production, sales, marketing, administration, legal or finance or whatever. It is also for people at all levels within an organisation. Business planning is not just for owners and directors: it's for anyone at any level who has responsibility for managing business resources, including the most junior of managers.

Finally, a few words of encouragement. You believe you have got a great business and you probably have. Your business plan is the final step in proving it to yourself and whoever else you have got to convince. Do it justice and prepare the best business plan you possibly can. Please don't rush it, and be prepared to visit some parts several times. I have seen hundreds of business plans and I can spot at a glance the plan crafted with effort and intimate knowledge of the business and its environment – it stands out head and shoulders above the rest. I hope this book helps you to get what you have set your heart on.

Planning – who needs it?

Chapter outline

Running a business is difficult at every stage of its life. It does not get any easier as your business grows. There are opportunities you may want to take up but there are dangers associated with each one. This chapter explains why you need a business plan and the benefits it will give your business. By the end of this chapter you will understand what sort of business plan you will need to prepare and the focus it will need. This chapter is essential reading for all business plan types.

Who needs a business plan?

I suppose the very brief answer to this question should be: *You* do. Despite my previous comments about my approach to DIY, I am convinced of the merits of planning, otherwise you might quite correctly question my right to have written this book on the subject. But you will be amazed by the gay abandon with which some people jump in without even a second thought.

I spend quite a lot of time working with bank managers, helping them to understand small business. They often ask me how I would convince someone of the need for a business plan. I take a purely selfish view on any venture that involves money – especially my own. I would want the maximum insurance I could have that my business idea was going to work and that I would not lose a penny of my own money or need any more than I had anticipated.

The business planning process gives me the chance to make my mistakes on paper before I am tempted to make them for real. It's not the first attempt at the business plan that is the right one – it may be the second or third after the earlier ones have failed closer scrutiny. It's at this point that I feel confident about my business idea and thank my lucky stars that no real harm has been done – I have made my mistakes on paper prior to getting on with it for real.

What is a business plan?

At this stage it is worth devoting a little time to explaining what a business plan is. *The Concise Oxford Dictionary* offers this definition of a plan: a detailed proposal for doing or achieving something. Basically a business plan should set out the business objectives; how and when these will be achieved; the resources that will be needed; the evidence that supports the assumptions. There is some common agreement on what it should contain, which we will of course cover later. How far ahead it looks will depend on its purpose – it should cover at least the period up to the achievement of the objective, which could be twelve months, two years, three years, or more than that.

How long your business plan will take to prepare is an unknown variable dependent on resources available: many hands make light work – do it alone and it will take you considerably longer. How long it should be is dependent on the audience for the business plan. My main experience is in the area of business plans designed to raise money. One plan at 120 pages was truly appalling – too much detail, and it bored the pants off me. I had lost the plot before the end. Another at thirty pages was right on the mark – concise but comprehensive.

Does a business plan help?

All the major banks and many learned institutions have conducted studies into the success and failure of businesses and have tried to establish a correlation between this and having or not having a business plan. A study by Cranfield University in 1990 showed that 75 per cent of businesses in their first year of existence did not have a business plan. The failure rate for this group of business was estimated to be about 40 per cent. On the other hand the same study showed that 95 per cent of businesses that had been trading for more than five years had a business plan. At the same time the failure rate for this group was estimated to be about 5 per cent. Now even I will be the first to agree that this does not prove that if you do not have a business plan you will go bust – but it does suggest that it helps and as your business gets more mature it will increase your chances of survival.

Stages of business development

The needs of a start-up business and a more mature business are quite different. In simple terms the business life cycle can be shown as follows:

- Start-up: During the first couple of years the issues are mostly to do with survival – finding customers (and keeping them), making sure products/services keep up with changing customer needs.
- Early years: During this period the main issues relate to consolidating the business – controlling the business, staff recruitment and retention, management structure.
- Growth and maturity years: During the rest of its life it faces the challenges of expansion – securing appropriate funding, moving premises, moving into new markets and new products, competing with bigger businesses, mergers/acquisitions, disposals, protecting its position.

As you can see, as a business matures, life becomes more complicated: it now becomes even clearer why it needs a business plan and why studies have shown that most of them have them.

The arguments against business planning

So why do so many businesspeople baulk at producing some sort of plan for their business? I suppose just for completeness I ought to run through the common arguments:

- 'I am not borrowing any money so I don't need a business plan.' Wrong. This is missing the main point of *why* you prepare a business plan. It's a chance to test out your business proposition on yourself and anyone else you can get to read it – before you start. If this process shows that your business proposition is sound, then congratulate yourself and proceed. If it shows that your idea is flawed then breathe a sigh of relief that you did not get started on it and blow all your money.

■ 'You cannot predict the future.' Partly correct. Probably the only thing you can't predict over the next twelve months is how much your customers will buy from you. During this time not too much else will change for most businesses – people, production, costs, financing requirements will be largely predictable. You can therefore model what your business will look like at a range of turnovers – we call this sensitivity analysis (more on this later). This will make sure that if sales do plummet you have a survival plan to handle it. Having no plan in periods of uncertainty sounds a bit like gambling to me – don't believe in it.

■ 'My business has been going for fifteen years. I don't need a business plan – I won't go bust.' A risky statement. I seem to recall the owners of the *Titanic* (the biggest and the best) saying something like that, and we all know what happened to that! But seriously, business failure hits mature-growth businesses – perhaps not as much as new businesses. Complacency can happen – the marketplace changes and customers no longer want your products. Technology moves on – just look at the speed of change in computers – and your product gets left behind. Sorry, but sound businesses need a business plan – they have got a lot to lose.

Have I convinced you yet? Are there still any doubters out there? Good. So what are the real benefits of having a business plan?

The benefits of business planning

Planning gives you a chance to make your mistakes on paper before you make them for real. You can test your business proposition before you commit to action.

Case study

If BMC had adopted this approach they may never have made the famous Mini car in 1959. It is believed that they thought they could make a profit by selling each car at under £500 and by working seven days a week with continuous shifts. In effect they were committing to a high-volume, low-price, high break-even-point strategy. At the time, informed commentators questioned how they could make a profit at such a low selling price – the truth was that they could not.

Unfortunately, for all sorts of reasons they could not produce at this high level and their production costs soared. It was rumoured at the time that it took BMC (later British Leyland, Austin Rover, and finally BMW) 25 years to make a profit out of the Mini. If they had only spent a bit more time at the planning stage doing some 'what-ifs', they would have been aware of the weaknesses of their proposed strategy.

Planning will enable you to identify all the resources you will need to successfully complete your plan. It will ensure you identify at the beginning how much cash you will need; how big a production/service facility will be required; how many people will be needed, etc. Too often these areas are neglected.

Case study

Some time ago I was advising a small Midlands-based specialist car-restoration business, which was planning its future strategy. Business was booming for them in the early 1990s. A quick forecast indicated that sales could easily double within the next twelve months. Further calculations showed that staff would have to grow from four full-time employees to eight to handle the extra workload. Additional equipment would be required – somewhere in the region of £20,000 would be needed to cover this.

The increased level of business would also mean higher levels of debtors requiring funding and increased purchases needing paying for. Finally, on taking an overview, it became quite clear that the existing premises would be too small. A move looked on the cards.

The two partners, who were husband and wife, spent hours agonising over the plan. They talked to me and they talked to their bank. Their bank manager was unwilling to lend them any more money to fund this growth. Whichever way they looked at it, the plan showed that they would need far more money than they had access to. It would be foolish to start this growth plan and know that they would run out of cash early on – the figures were staring them in the face. In the end they had to shelve the growth plan for that year – they could not afford it. Instead, that year, they put up their charge-out rates by 30 per cent – they were still busy, made far more profit and cash flow improved dramatically.

Preparing a business plan will get you into a new way of looking at your business. Planning is a continuous process that will ensure that your business is best suited to the changing business environment about it.

Case study

Each year Tim Holmes prepares a new business plan for his Coventry-based marketing communications business. He does not do it to borrow money from the bank. So why *does* he do it? It's part of an ongoing review of his business to see if anything is changing or needs to change. He looks both inside and outside the business. He talks to his customers, suppliers, staff, auditor and so forth. He wants their views. Is there anything that they are planning to do that will impact on his business plans? Does his service remain competitive and what his customers want? Does he need to change anything? It's part of his process of making sure his business stays in tip-top shape.

Apart from these benefits there are whole raft of others:

- Planning makes you feel more confident about the future – you are better prepared for some of the uncertainties ahead of you because you have thought about them in advance.

- Planning helps give you an invaluable tool to monitor and control your business by – if it is not in the plan then you should question why you are doing it. Is progress as good as planned? If not, why not? And what are you going to do about it?

- Planning is a great communication medium – involve others in it. This ensures staff are aware of company values, goals and objectives. And it will improve commitment to them.

- Planning will help improve company systems by identifying weaknesses during the process – make improvement a part of the business plan and commit resources to it.

- Planning takes away total reliance on 'gut feel' – it's OK to start with a hunch but back it up with unemotional and undeniable fact.

What sort of plan?

There should now be no question in your mind about the need for and benefits from having a business plan. The next question might be

'What sort of business plan do I need?' Well, it depends on what you want it for. I'm not trying to avoid the question – there's not a universal business plan that suits all business needs. Let me give you an analogy.

Most of us need a car to get to work, go shopping, take our families around, etc. If that's the case why don't car manufacturers today make just one model? Henry Ford did with great success seventy years ago by making the model T, available only in black. The problem is that we all have different needs and the car manufacturers have now moved into niche marketing, whereby they offer a vast array of different products. If you have five children then a people carrier is going to make more sense than a two-seater sports car. If you drive only two miles to work then you may be able to put up with some discomfort and a car that has poor fuel consumption – but would you feel the same way if you had to drive two *hundred* miles? Add to all this marketing hype, the need to impress, and other perceived social pressures, and it is small wonder that we agonise over buying cars.

So, as with buying a car, not all business situations are the same. If they were then one type of business plan would be sufficient. Most businesses have different needs at each stage and the plan must reflect this. Here are some common reasons for needing a business plan and the focus they will have:

To raise money

This could be if a business needs additional external funds to start up, expand or maybe acquire another. In this case the business plan will be sent to lenders, such as banks, charitable bodies, family and friends. It may also be sent to potential equity investors such as venture capital providers and business angels. Its purpose is to convince them the business proposition is sound and that any loans can be repaid comfortably on time. Also that dividends will be attractive and paid on time, and that any investment in this business will increase in value.

With this audience in mind the business plan will need to be very comprehensive and cover all aspects of the business. It will have a financial bias. Success in securing funding does not signify approval or responsibility by the lender – they have merely made the funds available. You will need the full business plan format as shown in Chapter Two and will need to follow every aspect of this book.

To obtain approval for a course of action

In this case it could be used internally to win approval from, say, the board of directors or the owner of the business. This plan prepared by internal management has as its purpose the diversion of internal resources to the project for which the business plan has been prepared. Approval by the board or owner will secure the funding and their acceptance that the plan is correct – they take joint responsibility.

It will be similar to the plan to raise money but the financial forecasts will be limited to profit and loss, cash flow and capital costs related to the project. You will not need the section on 'Funding required' but you will need a special section headed 'Payback'. Since those reading the plan will be familiar with the business, you will not need to include the section on 'Business and management'. You will need most of the business plan format as shown in Chapter Two but with minor modifications. You will still need to read all the chapters of this book but there will be signposts showing you how you need to approach certain parts.

Performance enhancement

Again, this might be used internally to convince the management team of the viability of the business idea. This is not used to secure funding or divert funds to a project. Its real purpose is to detail the proposed business objectives, and show how they can be achieved while subjecting them to full financial scrutiny. This type of plan is commonly presented by a director/owner to staff to communicate what the business is trying to achieve and their role in its success. Quite commonly it will detail manager/departmental responsibility through action plans and budgets – to secure managerial responsibility and commitment.

You will need most of the business plan format as shown in Chapter Two but with minor modifications. You will still need to read all the chapters of this book but there will be signposts showing you how you need to approach certain parts.

Enlist external support

This could be from suppliers, customers, etc. A business may want to obtain credit from its suppliers, trade with a large company or government body, or perhaps obtain a lease from a prospective land-lord. In this situation the other party is seeking to establish the credit-worthiness of the business, how professional it appears and whether it is likely to remain in business in two or three years' time. In this situation a full business plan as used for funding would be inappropriate – it would give too much away.

An outline business plan will be more appropriate outlining the history of the business: past financial performance; what the business does; some of its other customers and suppliers; details of its bankers and advisers; an outline of its current plans and how this supplier/customer fits into these. In this case the document may be only one to five pages long. This is a very special business plan and requires only the following sections:

1 Executive summary
2 Business and management – brief synopsis of this
3 Profit and loss forecast (restrict to details in executive summary)
4 Markets and competitors – brief synopsis of this
5 Production or service supply – brief synopsis of this
6 Appendices: audited accounts (most recent year)

A word of warning. You may start off with an initial reason for preparing a business plan, say to improve performance, but find that as you prepare it the events are changing. For example, as you outline your business idea it may become apparent that you don't have enough cash to complete the plan. Your business plan will then become one to raise cash and it will have a different target audience. In this case you will have to change the focus and to some extent the content of your business plan. Do keep an open mind as you are preparing your plan.

Hopefully, you can now see that there is not a universal business plan for all situations – they are all different because the target audiences are different. A plan for external funding will be a more serious tome requiring greater effort than a business plan outline for a supplier or customer – and the process will be different. Are you clear in your mind what sort of business plan you will need? You must be sure before you commence with your business plan.

Chapter summary

In this chapter we have learned that:

- Even if you are not borrowing money every business venture needs a business plan – if only to protect what it already has.

- Business plans are appropriate at every stage of business life – start-up, growth, maturity.

- There are numerous benefits from preparing a business plan – being able to make your mistakes on paper to prevent you from making them for real must be a key advantage.

- While the business plan is about your business, remember who you are preparing it for and why – this will determine what sort of plan is appropriate.

CHAPTER TWO

In search of the perfect business plan

Chapter outline

What goes into your business plan and the way you (and your team) prepare it is of vital importance. If you want it to stand out from the crowd you have got to convince your audience that you know what you are doing and that you are damn good at it. This chapter explains the steps you need to go through, the broad content of the business plan and the approach you must take to preparing and presenting it. By the end of this chapter you will know all you need to know so that you will be ready to write your business plan. This chapter is essential reading for all business plan types.

What makes a perfect plan?

For my sins I have read an awful lot of business plans in my role as a consultant and venture capitalist. Only a handful stick in my memory as being really good – most were pretty indifferent. I would like to briefly tell you about what was possibly the best (dare I say perfect?) business plan that I have reviewed.

Case study

Three young men in their early twenties had an idea to start up a nightclub in a disused cinema in Halifax. They had no money and limited management experience. Their business plan was not flashy, in fact it was printed using a very tired dot-matrix printer and amounted to about 25 pages in total. They wanted about £1 million through a combination of venture capital and 'soft loans' from the brewery. Based on this initial summary, your initial feeling might be, 'They've got no chance – no money, no trading history, no experience.'

So what made this a winning business plan? The proposition was good and I actually believed that they would deliver it. Their market analysis was superbly researched in a very low-key and practical way. They had visited all the local pubs and clubs (competitor analysis) to assess how busy they were and what they offered. They interviewed young people and asked them where they came from, how frequently they came for a night out in Halifax, why they used the various clubs and pubs, what they liked and disliked, what they would want from a new club (customer survey).

Their market analysis revealed that young people travelled in their masses to Halifax from as far away as Leeds and Manchester. It was a veritable Mecca of late-night drinking with a greater spend per head on alcohol than any other regional town or city. In addition, these same people wanted to dance but were largely unimpressed by the very downmarket discos offered by the town.

Their proposal was to provide a sophisticated London-style set-up with a different style of disco on each floor. They attracted the top award-winning DJs and of course offered late-night drinking and food – the food was required by the local magistrates before they would grant a late-night licence. The financial projections showed that no profit would be generated in Year 1, modest profit in Year 2 and very acceptable profits from Year 3 onwards. Included in their business plan were a very detailed operational plan and a costed programme for upgrading the nightclub to keep it up to date.

When the young management team came to make their presentation to me they brought an older man with them. He was introduced as the father of one of them and it was immediately apparent that he had acted as an adviser and had influenced their plans. As the non-executive chairman and managing director of a large quoted PLC he had vast experience to offer. As the meeting went on it became very clear that they were fully familiar with their business plan – it was all their own work – and they were able to answer all the questions we posed.

We had no hesitation in making our investment – we were totally convinced by their plan and their commitment to it. However, having made the money available, they had to get on and deliver against the plan. They had a very tough time – the magistrates took six months to grant a late-night drinks licence – but they opened up just about on time. The business was a great success – even now, some fifteen years later, I still meet people who rave about the Coliseum nightclub in Halifax.

Ten steps in business planning

So how will you ensure that you produce the best possible business plan? There are just ten steps – and you have already completed the first in the last chapter. Don't be put off – these are all necessary and, once completed, they will ensure that you have thoroughly thought through your business idea and provided the evidence to support it.

1 Why do you need a business plan and to whom will you present it (Chapter One)?

2 Explain your business idea and how well you have done so far (Chapter Three).

3 State your objectives and how you think you can deliver them (Chapters Three and Four).

4 Show how the numbers stack up – profitability, cash flow, funding (Chapters Five and Six).

5 Demonstrate your knowledge of the market, competitors and your product or services (Chapters Seven, Eight and Nine).

6 Identify the resources you will need to deliver your objectives – people, facilities, etc. (Chapters Nine and Ten).

7 Subject your plan to the reality test and make it recession-proof and bombproof (Chapters Two and Eight).

8 Set out how you are going to communicate the plan, implement it and control your business (Chapter Eleven).

9 Go through your business plan with a fine-tooth comb to make sure you have done everything (Chapter Twelve).

10 Deliver against the plan and if circumstances change or time passes by, start the process again (Chapter Twelve).

You will find that this book follows these steps by providing chapters that cover each of these ten steps. Follow the guidance in each of these and you will ensure that the content of your business plan is right up to the mark. Please remember that you must complete all of these steps. You may be tempted to skip steps 7, 8 and 9 either because you are in a hurry or sick of looking at your business plan – don't!

Outline of the business plan content

So far, so good – but what goes into the business plan? This will of course depend on its purpose, as was highlighted in Chapter One. The table that follows shows the main business plan section headings, what you should cover within each of these and where these are covered in this book. Regard these as the basic ingredients for the business plan – a bit like a menu from which you will pick and choose according to whether they are appropriate for your business. As a guide you will find that you will need all of these ingredients if your plan is to raise money, obtain approval for a course of action or improve performance – but some of the sections will have small variations in emphasis or content. If your business plan is to be used to enlist external support you will need only a handful of these ingredients. These individual requirements will be highlighted in each of the appropriate chapters.

Section heading	What is covered within this section	Which chapter(s) cover(s) this
Executive summary	Purpose of plan	Chapter 3
	Summarises the proposition	Chapter 3
	Outlines the rewards	Chapter 3
Business and management	When the business started and how it has performed so far	Chapter 4
	Current mission and objectives	Chapters 3 and 4
	Management team, key employees, structure	Chapter 4
	Legal structure of business and key shareholders	Chapter 4
	Professional advisers	Chapter 4
Financial forecasts	Profit and loss forecasts	Chapter 5
	Cash flow forecasts	Chapter 5
	Balance sheet forecasts	Chapter 5
	Break-even analysis	Chapter 5
	Key performance ratios	Chapter 5
	Assumptions	Chapter 5
	Sensitivity analysis	Chapter 5

Section heading	What is covered within this section	Which chapter(s) cover(s) this
Funding required	Purpose	Chapter 6
	Funding level required, timing and type of funding	Chapter 6
	The deal on offer/Payback	Chapter 6
Markets and competition	Market trends and projections	Chapter 7
	Sales forecast	Chapter 7
	Current and proposed customers	Chapter 7
	Competitor analysis	Chapter 7
Competitive business strategy	PEST – Environmental scanning	Chapter 8
	SWOT analysis	Chapter 8
	Contingency planning	Chapter 8
	Marketing strategy	Chapter 8
	Price, Promotion and Place	Chapter 8
	Channels of distribution	Chapter 8
Products or services	Description	Chapter 9
	Features and benefits	Chapter 9
	Comparison with competitors	Chapter 9
	Guarantees and warranties	Chapter 9
	Patents, trade marks, etc.	Chapter 9
	New products	Chapter 9
Production or service supply	The manufacturing process or service provision	Chapter 10
	Facilities and equipment needed	Chapter 10
	Capacity planning	Chapter 10
	Quality control	Chapter 10
	Sources of supply	Chapter 10
People	People requirements including recruitment and retention	Chapter 11
	Insurance	Chapter 11
Business controls	Financial systems	Chapter 12
	Other systems	Chapter 12
	Action plans	Chapter 12
Appendices	Action plans – detailed	Chapter 12
	CVs for management team	Chapter 4
	Audited accounts	Chapter 5
	Detailed forecasts	Chapters 5 and 7
	Detailed research on products, markets, competitors, etc.	Chapters 7 and 10
	Organisation chart	Chapter 11

Before you start to write your business plan

At this point you can start to think about researching and writing your business plan. But before you do start please consider the following pointers, which will help make your business plan stand out from the crowd. Your business plan must:

- Be fully researched and documented. Compare yourself to a solicitor in court. How much weight does his assertion have compared with a solid witness statement? Very little. Make sure that your business plan has been fully researched and that all the supporting information/evidence is included. If you make a statement such as 'Our customers will buy our new product in similar volumes to the old one' you are leaving yourself open to dispute. If, however, you make that same statement and back it up with documented market research – either independent or in-house (e.g. customer survey, competitive product analysis, etc.) – it is far more likely to be accepted. Do not include detailed market research, competitor analysis, product specifications and detailed financial forecasts/accounts within the main body of the business plan. Signpost them in the plan but include them in the appendices. This leaves the reader the option to refer to them if they want to – either at the time of reading or later.

- Be appropriate. The key thought that you must remember at all times as you prepare your business plan is 'Does the reader need to know this?' Don't let your enthusiasm carry you over the top. For example, if you are preparing your business plan to raise money it would be appropriate to include projected balance sheets and funding requirement. On the other hand, if your business plan is required by your landlord before he will grant you a lease (enlisting external support), this information is likely to be inappropriate, as would be market research, customer surveys, etc. Just tell them what they need to know.

- Be understandable. Don't let your business plan appear to be written in a foreign language. For example, if your product is quite complex and technical, do not assume that the reader has the same level of knowledge as you. Where appropriate, explain/define specialist terms that are unlikely to be known to the reader – either in the text itself or in a glossary in the appendices. Do not fall into using jargon specific to your business. However, by using clear English you should be able to explain even complex information to the average person. It is your responsibility to ensure that your business plan and all its complexities are understood by an intelligent reader who may not have any specific experience of your industry/product/service.

- Have passed the reality test. Don't let your business plan be another example of a spreadsheet exercise gone mad – this is where the profit and cash flow projections show amazing figures from day one. You may rightly be confident about your business proposition but your readers have something known as common sense – they can tell truth from fiction. In all probability they have seen similar businesses to yours before and they will know what is realistic and what is not. Don't forget that at some stage you have to deliver what your business plan outlines – don't make it impossible for yourself. All your statements and financial forecasts should be based on either past experience or supportable assumptions. At the same time don't make light of any business difficulties – they should be highlighted and a solution offered.

■ Have a smart and professional appearance. I know it sounds obvious, but don't let your quality business proposition be let down by its appearance.

Let's look further at this last point. If your business plan looks smart it will create a better impression on the reader – it will make them feel that you are smart, businesslike, well organised and so on. Fortunately, with the widespread availability of word-processing software, spreadsheets and business-planning software, laser printers and colour printing, there is no excuse for poorly presented material. At the very least your business plan should have:

■ A front cover. This tells the reader what they are looking at such as a 'Business Plan for XYZ Ltd for the years 2000 to 2005'. If the business plan has a specific purpose then this should be stated as well – for example, 'Proposal to raise £100,000 through the Loan Guarantee Scheme'. It should also state who has prepared the document – for example 'Prepared by John Smith, Managing Director'. It should bear the date of preparation of the document and a confidentiality statement to restrict its use – for example, 'Commercially Confidential Information – not to be distributed'. The front cover should be in a style that is appropriate to the business and should include any business logos and award symbols (e.g. ISO 9000, Queen's Award for Export, etc).

■ Contacts and advisers. It is quite common to give the name, address and telephone number for the key external advisers to the business on the next page. This could include accountants, auditors, solicitors, bankers and consultants. It would also be appropriate to include the business trading address, telephone number, fax number, website address and registered office. You may want to include a named contact within the business to whom further enquiries can be directed.

■ Contents page. The first real page of the business plan, which signposts to the reader where everything can be found within the pages. It should show the main sections together with the relevant page numbers for each.

- A main body. Every page should be A4 size, using good-quality paper. Send out originals (not photocopies) for review/approval, which should be spiral-bound within a clear plastic front and back, so that they can be read easily and are durable. If there are a significant number of appendices these should be bound separately – it reduces the size of the business plan proper and enables both to be read at the same time. Each page should be typed, rather than handwritten. Leave plenty of white space around the text – wide margins and double spacing will make it easier to read and less tiring. Use a plain font – Times Roman is a common choice – and use a legible type size: 10-point should do. Don't forget to number each page at the bottom.

- Clear style and accuracy. Use short sentences, short paragraphs, bullet points, headings and subheadings where appropriate – these make it easier to read. There should be no spelling mistakes in your document – so don't forget to use the spellchecker. Also, there should be no inaccuracies in your figures – if there is even one mistake the reader will be suspicious of every other figure in your plan. Check and recheck your business plan to make sure you pick up any mistakes. Get someone else to proofread it who has not been involved in its preparation – this is what publishers do to ensure their readers end up with as near perfect a script as possible.

How many pages?

The age-old question, to which the answer is: as few as possible. Try a little psychology in this respect. Whoever is going to read your business plan is going to be a busy person who has possibly seen a lot of such plans. You must give them sufficient information to make a decision – but they must not be left with too many unanswered questions.

A business plan can be made to appear shorter by splitting it into sections so the reader can pause and resume later, and by including separate appendices for the detailed financial projections, etc. By doing this you give the reader the chance to be selective and save time. However, as a general guide 20–40 pages is regarded as acceptable for a business plan to raise money and considerably fewer for most other purposes.

Who should write the business plan?

One person must have overall responsibility for it (usually the chief executive/managing director/owner), but it makes sense to delegate as much as possible to speed up the process and involve other management. By involving, for example, the marketing manager/director in preparing the marketing sector you will be drawing on their expertise and ideas as well as increasing their ownership of the resulting plan.

If you do involve others remember that you must first brief them – if you don't you may end up with a business plan that has sections on marketing, production, finance, etc. but they have no common purpose or style.

In a small company, business planning is usually a 'top-down' approach. The boss will set the overall business strategy and use lower managers to develop the detail of the plan. In very large organisations the approach is frequently 'bottom-up', whereby lower managers prepare plans for their units/departments, which are then incorporated into a master plan for the whole organisation. You should aim to involve some of both processes – set the main strategy and let managers prepare their plan within this.

Regardless of who writes the business plan, the chief executive/managing director/you must be able to answer every question asked – so you (or they) must be fully familiar with every word and figure within it.

Who shall I send it to?

If you are writing your business plan for internal purposes or for a known audience (e.g. a prospective landlord), then your task is quite straightforward. The recipients are known and it is just a case of ensuring that you have the correct name, title and address. If, however, the purpose of your business plan is to raise money, there is a far wider audience who you may want to contact – most of whom you do not know personally. You will do more harm than good by sending your business plan to all and sundry. Apart from the cost aspect, which can be considerable, you must consider the effect of your business plan falling into the wrong hands. You should do some research to find the right people to send it to – just as you would do if you were marketing your product/service.

Do not assume that banks and venture-capital organisations

operate in the same way. If you want to borrow money (debt) then approaching a bank is appropriate. If, however, you want someone to share in the risk of your business (equity) then venture capital is your first port of call – don't waste your time with the high street banks. However, not all venture capitalists operate in the same way. For example, some will not consider proposals below a certain value, say £250,000, while others will invest only in certain industries/technologies or stages of business development. Fortunately, there are organisations that can help point you in the right direction – some of these are shown in the appendices.

What to send

If you have done your research and identified just a small number of people who may be interested in your type of proposition then send them the full works. By this I mean the full business plan plus a personalised covering letter briefly outlining what you are after. If you want your business plan back after their deliberations you will need to mention this in your covering letter – otherwise they will throw it away.

If, however, your research throws up a larger number of possibles for your proposition, I would suggest a slightly different approach. In this case your approach is more speculative and I would suggest that you send out a covering letter and an outline of your business proposition – your executive summary could serve this purpose. Your letter should say that if they wish to receive the business plan this is available on request – that way only those people who are really interested will request and receive a business plan.

How to send it

You could spend a lot of time and effort in producing a top-notch plan and let yourself down by the way your plan appears to the recipient – late and bent. If your plan is going to a large number of people then you may have no option but to send it by first-class post. In this case ensure it arrives on time – at least a week before you hope to meet them. Also, mark the package as 'FRAGILE – DO NOT BEND' and send in a padded bag to improve its chances of survival. Use Special Delivery as a final bit of insurance to improve your chances of its being delivered.

A better method is to deliver the package in person – this should ensure it arrives in good condition and on time. Phone up first to find out whom you can leave it with – this will usually be the secretary of the ultimate recipient – and arrange a convenient time and place. Make sure that when you deliver the plan in person you are smartly dressed, just in case you accidentally bump into someone important.

How long the process will take after you have found a potential lender or investor is anybody's guess. If you are after a loan then this can usually be completed in a matter of just a few days or weeks at the longest. I recall venture capital deals being done within one month of receiving the business plan – but this was exceptional. My experience is that a typical venture capital deal will take between three and nine months to complete. Don't forget that, apart from yourself, accountants and lawyers will be involved (both sides), which will delay things. Also, a process known as 'due diligence' will have to be carried out – this is where every statement in your business plan will be checked and 'warranted' by you to be correct.

A word of warning. Raising money is a time-consuming and distracting business. Don't forget that you still have a business to run and that if you take your eye off the ball your business will suffer. I have seen several cases where a healthy business has nearly gone bust during the funding negotiation/completion process – the management was so involved in this process that they neglected the day-to-day running of the business. Don't let this happen to you.

Presenting the business plan

Treat this meeting as an examination because that is exactly what it is – an examination of you and your business proposition. I would suggest that you focus on three things.

1 How you want to run the meeting

It's your day, so take control. If you are seeing the bank manager you have probably got one hour at the most – a little longer if you are seeing a venture capitalist. Find out in advance how long the meeting will last. Plan both the time and the content. My experience is that the best use of a one-hour slot is as follows:

0–20 minutes: Introductions and outlining your business plan
21–50 minutes: Discussion and answering questions on the business plan
51–60 minutes: Concluding discussions based around decision

Use this as a guideline. Do not talk for too long – watch out for the body language of your audience. Yawns and closed eyes should tell you it's time to move along more quickly and get them more involved. If you have taken your management team along with you, work out in advance how they will be introduced and what they will do. They don't all have to present – they may be there to answer technical questions. If you are the chief executive/managing director/owner then you should introduce your team, explaining how you would like the presentation to proceed. Make sure that you conclude your team's presentation.

If you get nervous at the prospect of making presentations, get help. There are plenty of good books on presentation skills. Speak clearly and try to be as relaxed and as natural as possible. Don't appear cocky, overconfident or grovelling – it won't work. Also, do try a dummy run of your presentation (and answering likely questions) before you do it for real – and possibly make mistakes.

2 Questions and answers

Expect questions and be prepared for them – it's normal. Don't assume that questions are a criticism of your business plan – they are not. You will certainly be questioned about the contents of the plan – these may be used to check facts, make clear areas of uncertainty or deal with omissions. Other questions may be used to clarify additional points you have mentioned in your presentation. If you are fully familiar with your business and the business plan, then most questions should be answerable.

However, there may be some questions that you cannot answer – for example, some commercial factor that you did not know about or may have overlooked. Do not try to bluff it out – this is a high-risk strategy.

If there is a problem within your business plan and it is highlighted, acknowledge it and outline how you will deal with it. An acceptable response might be to say, 'I don't know the answer to that but I will find out and let you know.' If you are not certain how you might deal with the problem, ask the questioner how they might suggest you dealt with it. Keep your answers short and to the point.

If it seems that there are no further questions or you are running tight on time, do move the meeting along with 'If there are no further questions . . .' or 'We're running a bit short on time and there are some other important areas that we need to cover so can we . . .?'

3 Appearance and timing

Wear something that makes you feel comfortable and is appropriate to the meeting. For example if you were a plumber and you were meeting the bank manager to arrange a small overdraft you would not need to wear a suit – if you did, it might make both you and the bank manager feel uncomfortable. On the other hand if you were a furniture designer and you were making a presentation to a venture capitalist to raise, say, £5 million, then you would be expected to wear a suit. The impression that you must give is that you care – don't turn up in your worst work clothes.

Make sure you leave yourself enough time for important meetings like this. Allow plenty of time for travel and getting lost – especially if you are going somewhere you don't know. Also do try to arrive at least five or ten minutes early so you can relax and be in the right frame of mind for the meeting. If there are more than one of you making the presentation, arrange to meet the others at a convenient place (a café, say) close to the meeting half an hour before your appointment. This way you can be sure you all arrive on time together or at least be aware of any unforeseen problems before you enter the meeting.

A couple of final points on the business plan presentation. While it is your day, don't forget to observe the usual social niceties. At the start of the meeting wait to be shown to your seat(s) and do wait to be invited to start your presentation. Your audience should have received your business plan in good time and have read it – but do not assume this. Ask them at the start of the meeting if they have read the plan. If they have not you will have to contain your disappointment or anger and spend a bit more time on this area in your presentation.

If at the end of the meeting they have not given you a decision don't be afraid to ask them 'What happens next?' so that you are aware of the follow-up procedure. You should also ask them to indicate when you will receive a decision and how it will be communicated to you. It is always worthwhile to send a polite letter to the recipient of your plan thanking them for their time and saying you look forward to receiving their decision soon. Don't be afraid to phone them up if you have not heard their decision within, say, two weeks.

Of course, your intention is to ensure that your business plan is successful and that the outcome is as you hope. In which case you will receive an offer from the bank or the venture capital house or acceptance from the board. You can thank them politely, go out and celebrate – but do not forget that you have got to get down to business and deliver against the business plan.

The rest of this book looks at putting together the evidence for your business plan – you might call it putting the flesh on the bones of the business plan that is starting to form in your head.

Chapter summary

In this chapter we have learned that:

- There is a recognised process to preparing a business plan that comprises ten steps – all of which must be completed.

- The content of the business plan is fairly standard – there are just some changes of emphasis and you may not need all of it for your purposes.

- Before you start to write, think about the qualities your business plan will need – researched and documented, appropriate, understandable, passed the reality test, smart and professional.

- The presentation of your business plan must be first-class – don't let your written plan down by your poor presentation.

CHAPTER THREE

Hey, you! What do you want?

Chapter outline

I know it's common sense but you have got to have objectives, otherwise how will you know when you have achieved what you are setting out to do? Not only that but your objectives have got to make sense – something you can achieve, not the frustratingly impossible. Finally, you need to capture your whole business plan in just two pages and present it to your reader so they are excited and want to read the rest. This chapter tells you all you need to know about setting down SMART (specific, measurable, achievable, realistic, timed) objectives and writing your executive summary. By the end of this chapter you will have told the reader why you have prepared this business plan – all he or she has to do now is read the plan to see how you are going to achieve your objectives. This chapter is essential reading for all business plan types.

Which parts of the business plan are covered in this chapter?

Section heading	What is covered in this section	Full business plan (external – raising money)	Business plan (internal – performance enhancement)	Business plan (internal – board approval)	Summary plan (external – lease, suppliers, etc.)
Executive summary	Purpose of plan	Yes	Yes	Yes	Yes
	Summarising the proposition	Yes	No	Yes	Yes
	Outlining the rewards	Yes	No	Yes – but restricted to payback	No
	Current mission and objectives	Yes	Yes	Yes	Yes

Section heading	What is covered in this section	Full business plan (external – raising money)	Business plan (internal – performance enhancement)	Business plan (internal – board approval)	Summary plan (external – lease, suppliers, etc.)
Comments	This section sells your plan – so make it short and snappy.	This is a finance bid aimed at people who don't know the business.	Remember that this is just to guide and motivate.	This is a finance bid aimed at people who already know the business.	This is just a bare-bones summary – don't reveal too much because it is not needed.

Where do you want to go?

Up to now the focus has been historical: what you have done to date. Let's start to look forward to the exciting part: where do you want to go? I recall frequent discussions with clients when I would ask them where they saw themselves and their business in, say, twelve months' time. The usual answer was 'I don't know.'

Case study

Some years ago I asked this same question of Bill Worrall, who was then attending a programme for owner-managers at Warwick University's Centre for Small and Medium Sized Enterprises. Bill was a most delightful engineer of the old school – he loved solving customers' problems for them.

His business, George Worrall Engineering Limited, had been started by his father but was now run by Bill. The business, which was typical of a lot of family businesses, was sound but relied on Bill – too much, in my opinion. He was just one of a dozen businesses on the programme and they had all been challenged to tell the group where they wanted to go – both on a personal level and with the business. 'OK, Bill,' I said, 'it's your turn – where do you want to be in twelve months' time?' To be honest his response was a bit middle-of-the-road and seemed to me to lack real conviction – no passion to it. I forget the detail of it but in essence he wanted to sort out a few marketing issues and improve profitability a bit.

Unconvinced by Bill's answer, I asked him where he wanted to be in five years' time. Quite suddenly there was a real outpouring of his inner feelings. A passion returned to his voice and he said, 'I want to be out of this bloody business – I feel trapped and I have had enough.' He added, 'I want to sell the business because there are other things I want to do with my life.' Suddenly a real purpose returned to the discussion. Bill knew now what he needed to do with his business – there were two key objectives:

1 He needed to make the business independent of him within the next two years. This meant creating managers and supervisors to take over from him.
2 He needed to make the business attractive so that he had the option to sell it within three to five years. This meant making it seriously more profitable (as well as independent of him).

Suddenly, by taking the longer view, a clarity returned that spelled out what needed to be done in Years 1, 2, 3, 4, etc.

So I would suggest that you look at the long term first to establish your business objectives. As a colleague of mine used to say, 'If you want to know what to do next year you should first look forward to where you want to be in five years' time and work backwards to establish the key milestones you will need to pass to achieve that.'

Many business plans are too short-term in their view. Quite frequently their objectives are associated with sales and profit growth over the next one or two years; getting out of a poor cash position; obtaining a lease; getting support from the main board, and so on. Don't get me wrong – there is nothing wrong with these objectives per se, but they frequently ignore the long-term objectives. Perhaps I can give you a more tangible example to illustrate this.

Under normal circumstances a healthy-growth business would prepare a business plan that focused on growth. This plan (Plan A) might show increased sales, investment in facilities, development of new products/services, recruitment of more staff. As a result of this plan, cash and profitability is likely to suffer in the short term as the process of growth takes place. However, after two or three years, this plan will show improved profits and cash – a worthwhile result. Let's say that over three years net profit is projected to improve from £100,000 per year to £133,100 (an average of 10 per cent per annum).

However, let's add a vital bit of information. Suppose the owner of this business wants to sell up in five years' time for £1 million so that he can pursue another business idea. He has been advised that his business will need to be generating net profits of closer to £200,000 per year to achieve this sale. To meet this objective the business will need to improve net profits by closer to 15 per cent per annum. To achieve this quite a different plan is required (Plan B) – one that maximises profits. This plan might include increasing selling prices, improving production efficiency, cutting overheads, tight cash management.

Hopefully, you see my point. You cannot set a plan for Year 1 until you know what you want to achieve by Year 5. Had this business set out on Plan A it would have done well but failed to meet the longer-term objective of getting the business ready for a £1 million sale.

Business and personal objectives

I implore you at this stage not to ignore personal objectives – do not make yourself a martyr to your business. Yes, you do need to be fully committed to your business, but do know when to stop, or at least take your foot off the pedal. In the short term you can work days and nights for your business but do this for ever and you will sacrifice your family life and your health. How do I know this? I have done it and paid the consequences: health, wealth and wife. However, I have plenty of clients who have got the mix of work and play entirely right.

Case study

A good friend of mine, Ian Dunwoody, is the owner and chief executive of Travel Management Group PLC. Over the years he has built it up to a turnover that is now approaching £50 million – which has made his company one of the largest independent travel businesses in the UK. Until recently I found it almost impossible to contact him because he was always away on business. It took a combination of events to get him to re-evaluate his personal and business objectives.

Business was good, his staff is first-class and on a day-to-day basis his business did not need him. A series of factors persuaded him to change his way of life. He was, even by his own admission, not looking after himself properly. Good food and wine, frequent travel and lack of exercise had taken its toll. Pressures at work for office space gave him the golden opportunity – he now works from home. He has all the benefits of modern communications to support him but on a day-to-day basis he can work, be with his wife and pursue other interests. His quality of life has improved immensely and his business has not suffered at all. When I spoke to him last he said that he and his wife were going abroad for a month – to a health resort. To me it looks like his business and personal life are in perfect harmony.

So please make sure that your personal and business objectives are compatible. It may not be possible for you to do what Ian did – your business may still need you to drive it forward. However, your plan should include a busy, motivated, healthy you – otherwise it has little chance of success. I would like to recommend a book that has had a profound effect on me and many of my friends and clients – *The Seven Habits of Highly Effective People*, written by Stephen R Covey. This has sold in excess of 10 million copies so I would suggest that it has a powerful message.

SMART objectives

People frequently talk about short- and long-term objectives. Unfortunately this is all a matter of perspective and varies from person to person and business to business. For example, if I said to Mark, my son, that next month we were going to watch Leeds United play AC Milan I know his response would be, 'Great, but that's ages away!' whereas from my viewpoint that is just around the corner. We are stuck with the labels 'short-term' and 'long-term' – but you decide how you interpret these for your business and state clearly the actual time period involved – for instance, within two years.

There is, however, common agreement on how they should be set down. The common sense is that your business objectives should be clear and unambiguous. In fact they should be SMART objectives:

> ■ **Specific.** Include objectives that are specific. Suppose your objective is to grow sales faster than last year (which was, say, 10 per cent), then this could cover anything from 11 per cent to 1,000 per cent – which is not very specific. You should be quite specific: for example, 'Our objective is to grow sales by 15 per cent per annum.'
>
> ■ **Measurable.** Your objective must be capable of measurement. Don't include objectives like biggest, best, fastest in the UK/world,

etc. because these are not usually measurable. Include measures such as sales, gross margin, net profit, and market share – these are clear, unambiguous and easily measured.

■ **Achievable.** The objective must be capable of being achieved with the resources you have available. For example, if your output capacity is 100,000 units a year, do not set an objective that requires 200,000 units a year of output – unless your plan shows where this extra capacity will come from.

■ **Realistic.** As well as being achievable, the objective must be realistic. For example, if your sales growth has historically been 15 per cent no one will believe your objective of 30 per cent annual sales growth – unless you can show what you are going to do differently to achieve this (and make it convincing).

■ **Timed.** You must say when you will achieve the object, e.g. within the next twelve months, two years. Don't use terms such as 'in the short term', 'near future', 'in the long term' – these mean something different to everyone and are far too vague.

Having set your SMART objectives you will need to say how these will be achieved. This is what the rest of your business plan is all about. Later you will need to set out action plans, which assign personal responsibility to individual management team members for delivering the business plan objectives.

Common business objectives

You may feel that I am placing a lot of emphasis on objectives. I am. They are the core of your business idea and inextricably linked with your mission. As such, they must be valid, sensible and appropriate for your business at this stage. Get them wrong and you will experience frustration and, ultimately, failure.

Case study

I recall speaking with Dave Simmonds, who ran a business that had a serious challenge ahead of it. One of his major suppliers had indicated that it was going to cease supplying a product that was very important to the manufacture of his business' product. It was nothing personal (said his supplier), but, because the UK market was very small and really was not sufficiently profitable for a large multinational, it had decided to stop supplying the UK.

This posed a real problem for Dave. In his darkest hours he saw it as threatening his company's very existence. The real truth was that it was a real pain but if sufficient thought were applied to the problem a range of solutions could be found, which, although not ideal, would provide an adequate solution.

Dave was in the process of preparing a new business plan with just one objective. He was going to find a way to formulate and produce a copy of the product he was going to be unable to buy. It involved recruiting a chemist, setting up a laboratory facility and spending time and money on inventing the due-to-disappear ingredient.

This was an area in which he had no experience at all. His business was essentially a joinery operation – it made and installed industrial sinks and work units. At the same time he was going to run an enterprise for which he did not have a current business plan. Over the next twelve months that I had regular contact with Dave I saw the frustration that he was going through. Finding the missing ingredient became an all-consuming passion – probably to the detriment of his business. In all the time I knew him he never came up with his own version of the product.

Don't make the same mistake that I believe my friend did. If your main business objectives include any of these listed below then you are probably on the right track:

- Increasing shareholder value
- Increasing dividend pay-outs
- Improving profitability
- Increasing market share
- Making the business secure (stopping it from going bust)
- Providing profitable employment for your staff
- Personal satisfaction (as long as the business thrives)
- Meeting some charitable, religious or altruistic objectives
- Getting the business ready for sale
- Getting that lease, contract, etc.

The hierarchy of goals

In this book we will talk about missions, objectives and action plans – but how do they all fit together, and what is their relevance to the planning process? They are all part of a hierarchy of goals. Starting at the highest level:

- **Mission statements:** These are direction statements, which give direction and focus to everyone in the business. Try not to do too many things but do make sure that your mission leaves a big enough market in which to trade profitably.
- **Objectives:** These follow on from mission statements and are the start of the planning process. As we have seen, these state what you want to achieve and when – how big, etc.
- **Tasks:** These follow on from objectives and are the high-level activities that need to be achieved to meet the objectives. For instance, what we need to do over the next twelve months.
- **Action plans:** These follow on from the tasks and are the low-level activities that need to be carried out to fulfil the tasks. For example, what we do on Monday morning.

Missions and objectives are often referred to as 'what' statements and tasks and action plans are 'how to' statements. Perhaps a brief example can help to illustrate the whole hierarchy.

Case study

Ken Lewis Engineering was quite clear about its mission statement, objectives, tasks and action plans.

- **Mission:** We aim to be a profitable, high-quality, second-tier supplier of plastic fittings to the motor industry and a primary supplier to the packaging industry.
- **Objective:** In the next twelve months we want to increase turnover to £750,000 and make a net profit of 10 per cent on sales.
- **Tasks:**
  1 Work with our customers to improve communications and scheduling.
  2 Improve cash flow by improving cash collection and managing supplier payments better.
  3 Improve networking to identify further potential customers.
  4 Improve workshop efficiency.
- **Action plan:**
  1 Monday morning – Ken to phone friends/business colleagues/customers to find out if they have any more work or can put him in touch with anyone who may have.

> 2 Monday morning – Ben to start building a spreadsheet on which he can schedule customer jobs to each machine and plan/monitor workshop performance.
>
> 3 Monday afternoon – Jan to prepare a three-month cash-flow forecast and use it to chase debtors and pay suppliers.

Now can you see how they all fit into place? I often find that business plans are weak on mission statements, reasonable on objectives, and ignore tasks and action plans. A business plan has no value unless it is implemented – it's just hot air unless you carry it out. I would, however, mention that, if the purpose of your business plan were to obtain approval for a course of action or to enlist external support, I would not expect to see tasks and action plans included.

Executive summary – the essence of your business plan

If your objectives are agreed, then now you need to start to sketch out how you are going to achieve them. In anatomy terms I would regard this as the skeleton around which the rest of the business plan forms the flesh. This skeleton, which is called the executive summary, is, as its name implies, a brief summary of your business plan.

You should start to think about it before you write your business plan (to give you focus) and revisit it when you have completed your plan (to ensure you haven't changed your mind). It is absolutely key to the success of your plan because it is the first thing (after the contents page) that your reader will see. This is the sales pitch that must say to the reader, 'Wow! This is the best business idea I've ever seen and I can't wait to find out more.' Get the executive summary wrong and you will lose your reader.

When I was working as a venture capitalist I would be bombarded with up to ten business plans a day. Time was at a premium – if I read them all thoroughly my day would be gone. My general approach was to (a) see the thickness of the business plan – and noticeably groan if it was too big – and (b) quickly read the executive summary to see if it was going to grab my attention. If I liked the look of the executive summary I would usually read on with enthusiasm. If I did not like it I seldom read the rest of the plan. Please take heed of this warning –

make it short and snappy. My recommendation is that it should be no longer than two pages.

So how do you write this key part of your business plan? Remember what I said earlier – this is the essence of your business plan, a sort of business plan in miniature. It should have purpose and be entirely positive right from the start. Your first sentence should tell the reader exactly what you want: for instance, 'Beechwood Enterprises Limited is seeking to raise £1 million of equity funding to fund its expansion into the US market. In return it is offering the investor a 20 per cent share in the company . . .' Now hit them with the rest of the plan and include:

- The management team (remember, people invest in people)
- Your products and services and why they are special (because that's the next thing that people invest in)
- Why your customers will buy your products/services
- Your business objectives and a brief outline of the strategies you will employ to achieve them
- A summary of the key financial forecasts
- How much money is required, how it will be used, and what the investor/lender will get in return

Draft out the executive summary before you start the main body of the business plan and refine it as the plan progresses. Revisit it when your business plan is complete – just to make sure it is consistent with the rest of the plan (especially the financial forecasts and money requirements). There is nothing worse than the executive summary stating that profits will be £X,000 in Year 1 and the financial forecast in the main body of the business plan showing something different.

Case study

The following is an example of an executive summary that I recently read.

Autoclean Limited have been trading profitably for 5 years and are seeking to borrow £100,000 under the Small Firms Loan Guarantee Scheme over a period of 5 years to fund the production of a new mobile coach wash system (CoachWash System™) for which they have secured advance orders of £350,000 (14 units).

The CoachWash System™ is an important advance in mobile coach-cleaning systems because it uses 50 per cent less water and 30 per cent less cleaning chemicals than its nearest competitor whilst having a significant price advantage. Overall this should enable most coach operators to save some 40 per cent on their cleaning costs. Our initial tests carried out on customers' coaches have proven to their satisfaction that the system cleans quicker and better than any other system currently in the marketplace.

In the UK alone there are 350 coach operators, of whom 20 per cent currently use 750 automated coach-cleaning systems. Our initial marketing has revealed that some 40 coach operators have expressed a strong interest in our new CoachWash System™ and would purchase one within the next 18 months. We would hope that as we start to deliver the new systems we can demonstrate to those using manual cleaning methods the cost effectiveness of using our new system thus securing more sales.

The new CoachWash System™ has been designed entirely in-house by Mark Chapman, our technical manager. Our own production team made the initial pre-production prototype with the help of outside consultants part funded by the DTI. We now require £35,000 to set up the initial production line modifications with the remaining £65,000 being required for tooling and initial materials to make the first batch of 5 units.

Our objective is to sell 20 units in year 1 and 40 units in year 2, which would amount to 8 per cent of the installed automated coach-cleaning systems in the UK. We are currently number two in the marketplace with our current coach-cleaning system.

Our financial forecasts show that this new product will account for £500,000 (25 per cent of all sales) during the first 12 months. This has been based on selling 20 units at £25,000 each – for which we have already secured orders for the first 8 months' production. The new product will have a gross profit of 42 per cent and even in year 1 will make a profit contribution of £160,000 after other marketing, sales and distribution costs and additional financing charges. Other products will account for £2 million turnover and yield net profits of £300,000.

I don't hold this out to be a perfect example of an executive summary but it certainly grabbed my attention – I wanted to read the rest of the business plan because I felt convinced that the business idea was hugely profitable, capable of being done by this team, and offered an almost cast-iron guarantee that the loan would be repaid. In fact, after reading this executive summary I was almost writing out the cheque.

Chapter summary

In this chapter we have learned that:

- You need to think five years ahead to make sure that your objectives in Years 1, 2, 3 and 4 will get you to the right position.

- Your objectives must be SMART – then you will be able to tell whether you have achieved them. Make sure you have included them in your business plan.

- Missions, objectives, tasks and action plans are all intertwined – they start and end the planning process.

- The executive summary is key to your success – it must grab the reader's attention and make them want to read the rest of the business plan. Start it now and revisit it at the end of the business planning process.

CHAPTER FOUR

What is it you do – and how well do you do it?

Chapter outline

You know your business and what it can do, but how do you communicate this to your target audience? Don't assume that they know anything – tell them about your business and what it has achieved to date. This includes information such as financial performance to date, the key people involved in your business, the legal structure of your business. This chapter explains what you need to tell them about your business as a way of setting the scene before you outline your business proposition. By the end of this chapter you will have told the reader all they need to know to prepare them to read the main body of your business plan. This chapter is essential reading for all business plan types.

Which parts of the business plan are covered in this chapter?

Section heading	What is covered in this section	Full business plan (external – raising money)	Full business plan (internal – performance enhancement)	Full business plan (internal – board approval)	Summary plan (external – lease, suppliers, etc.)
Business and management	When the business started and how it has performed so far	Yes	Yes	No – they already know this	Yes
	Current mission and objectives	Yes	Yes	Yes	Yes
	Management team, key employees, structure	Yes	Yes	Yes	No

Section heading	What is covered in this section	Full business plan (external – raising money)	Full business plan (internal – performance enhancement)	Full business plan (internal – board approval)	Summary plan (external – lease, suppliers, etc.)
	Legal structure of business and key shareholders	Yes	No	No – they already know this	Yes
	Professional advisers	Yes	No	No	Yes
Comments	This section sets the scene.	This is a finance bid aimed at people who don't know the business.	Remember that this is just to guide and motivate.	This is a finance bid aimed at people who already know the business.	This is just a bare-bones summary – don't reveal too much because it is not needed.

Reviewing the current situation

You may recall the old Irish saying, 'If you want to go there, sir, I wouldn't start from here.' There is much to commend this simple statement when looking at your business and the proposed plan that you may have for it. You can't change the past but do recognise that it will affect the present and the future.

Case study

Let me give you an example from a business that was in the travel industry. Historically the business had specialised in tours 'back to the home country' for the Irish community living in the Midlands. A family-run business, it had done modestly well over the years but with the second generation now in control it wanted to do bigger and better things.

The new managing director, Steve, had decided that there were two fronts on which he wanted to attack. He wanted to establish a London office, which he hoped would capture more of the Irish market in the capital. He also wanted to set up a business travel facility because he believed there were lots of businesses locally that he could be servicing without any further costs. On the face of things this looked like a sound business strategy – it certainly seemed to have the potential to make a lot of money.

I suggested that Steve take a little time out to review the situation. 'Why don't we see what sort of shape the business is in for this big new adventure?' I offered.

Together we looked back over the last few years to see how well the business had done in terms of financial performance, service delivery, and marketing and people issues. Well I won't bore you with all the details but it was quite revealing. We gave each of these areas a score out of 10 (1 = low, 10 = high) and made a few comments. The result was a bit like an end-of-term report.

Criteria	Score	Comments
Financial performance	4	Lack of growth in profitability. Poor track record of investment. No significant cash resources
Service delivery	5	Customers come back. No new product offerings in last five years.
Marketing	3	Don't do much.
People issues	5	People don't leave. No management below family directors.

Steve was forced to agree that this was a pretty ordinary business. It had no experience of product or service innovation and it had no cash to spend even if it had any ideas. Overall, the conclusion was that this was a very steady sort of business that had no experience of change and was not in a strong financial position.

How, then, would this business cope with two new business ideas, both of which would require people, money and a new service – the things that were not strengths to this business? The answer was staring Steve in the face – it would not be able to manage *one* of these opportunities, let alone both. The answer was clearly not expansion but consolidation – get the basic business right before moving on to greener pastures. Perhaps not what Steve wanted to hear but the right plan for his business.

It's time to subject your business to a similar review – a review of your business's history and position to date. This will have two benefits:

1   It will enable the reader of your business plan to get a potted history of your business so that they can understand what you

do and how well you do it, and see how your new business plan fits in with this.

2 It will remind you of where you have come from and help assess how strong your current business is.

I will give you fair warning here and now. If your business is weak then growth through rapid expansion or diversification is not a valid option – you will almost certainly run out of cash. Your business proposition should build on your business strengths or be able to demonstrate how it will make itself change to accommodate expansion or diversification.

Describing your business

This is the easy bit – describing your business. If your business plan is for internal use this will be a summary section because your readers will already know this. This section is primarily to bring an external audience, such as bankers, venture capitalists, a landlord, up to speed, and it is needed, whatever stage your business is at – be it a start-up or a fifty-year-old public company. This section of information should not be contentious. Here is a brief checklist of what you will need to cover:

1 Basic business information:

- Name of business (and when it was started)
- Legal status (sole trader, partnership, limited company, etc.)
- Authorised and issued share capital (and major shareholders)
- Registered office and trading addresses
- Company registration number
- Professional advisers (bankers, lawyers, accountants, etc.)

2 Current mission and objectives.
3 The management, key employees and organisation structure.
4 Milestones and financial performance to date.

1 Basic business information

Name of business

You should choose a business name that is appropriate to your business and will not place any limitations in the foreseeable future. It is common practice for actors and other performing artists to choose a name that fits the image that they are trying to portray. John Wayne was well known for his tough cowboy image but had he used his real name, Marion Morrison, it is unlikely that he would have enjoyed as much success.

Case study

Mike Evans already had a very successful public-relations agency called Agrafax, which, as its name implies, worked predominantly within the agriculture industry sector. In fact the business was highly regarded and considered by many to be the market leader in this sector.

Unfortunately, this success was also a problem: it was restricting his ability to grow the business. By acting for one client he was effectively barred from working for their competitors in that industry sector. He realised that future growth was likely to be achieved in other industry sectors and that the Agrafax name would not be so useful – it might in fact hold them back because of its perceived associations.

Eventually the name the Mistral Group Ltd was chosen. The word 'mistral' in itself was quite neutral and had no association with any industry sector. Use of the word 'group' implied size, which was helpful in approaching large organisations.

Over the next few years the Mistral Group was very successful in entering other industry sectors. There was no impact on the existing agriculture business as the name Agrafax was retained as a division of the Mistral Group Ltd.

If you have to choose a business name, either because you are starting up a new business or have decided that your existing business name could use a new image, bear in mind the following. Your business name should be consistent with:

- Who you are
- What your business does
- How you go about things

Dyno-Rod, Prontaprint, Budget Car and Van Rental are all good examples of business names that describe what these businesses do. Quite frequently a one-line slogan or strap line is added to tell the world how they go about things. Pickfords, who are probably the biggest and best-known removal business in the UK, have added the slogan 'The Careful Movers' – designed to inspire confidence. Kwik-Fit boast that 'You can't get better than a Kwik-Fit fitter'.

When you have chosen your business name do make sure that you can use it – especially before you get your stationery printed. There are some names that you cannot normally use because they are deemed to be 'controlled'. Examples of these are the words 'royal', 'international', 'bank'. You will need to obtain permission to use these. You cannot use a name that is misleading, obscene, offensive or illegal. For example, if you wanted to use the name the Enterprise Group Ltd you would have to be able to show that it is in fact a group of companies under common ownership.

You will also need to make sure that if you are trading as a limited company your intended name is not being used by another. Fortunately, the Registrar of Companies will not allow you to do this – but check with them first to ensure your chosen name is available. There is normally no problem in using your own name for trading purposes. However, if you choose to trade using a name other than your own you must indicate who owns the business. Contact the Department of Trade and Industry or Companies Registration Office for further assistance (see appendices for contact information).

Legal status

Most businesses trade as 'sole traders' but there are alternatives that should be considered. The main types of business entity are:

- Sole trader
- Partnership
- Co-operative
- Limited liability company

But which is best for you? This will depend on how many people are involved; how much risk you are prepared to take; whether you need to raise equity (risk) funding; how much formality you are pre-pared to tolerate. To see which is best for you review the options below.

Sole trader

As already mentioned, this is the most common type of business entity. You just start trading either under your own name or a suitable trading name. All you need to do is contact the Department of Social Security to pay your Class 2 National Insurance contributions. You should also contact your local tax office to inform them of your business. They will want to know such things as: when you started trading; your proposed business year end; your accountants' (if any) details. You should also be aware that if your turnover is likely to be above about £52,000 per annum you would need to be registered for VAT purposes.

Pros

- Easy to set up with very little formality (especially if you are not VAT-registered)
- No accounts to be audited – submit directly to Tax Office
- You are your own boss
- Taxation is usually quite straightforward

Cons

- Because you are the business you are personally liable for all its liabilities – this means your personal assets are at risk
- Access to external funding is limited to loans – cannot issue shares to raise equity (risk) funding

Partnership

This one is rather cruelly referred to as the worst of both worlds and not liked by many advisers. A partnership is a collection of sole traders and really shares the same legal status as such. A partnership can be formal, whereby there is a written partnership agreement, or informal, whereby the agreement is tacit or oral. In theory, by getting together with like-minded individuals you will have access to more capital; additional skills to use in the business; someone to run the business if you are temporarily unable to work.

There are some points that must be remembered when considering the partnership option:

- You are jointly liable for the actions of your partners. If they make a mistake and the business suffers a financial loss as a result, all the partners are treated as if they had made the mistake – even if they did not all know of or agree to the action. Your personal assets could be used to pay the business debts.

- If one of the partners becomes bankrupt their creditors can seize their share of the partnership. This may mean that the existing partners may have to wind up the business or take on loans to pay out the bankrupt partner's share of the business.
- The death of one partner will bring the partnership to an end – it cannot continue with just the remaining partners.
- If you want to leave a partnership it is difficult, and your liability can be continuing unless you take formal steps to notify your business contacts and legally bring the partnership to an end.

Partnerships are covered by the Partnership Act 1890. However, this merely provides a fall-back position for those situations where a formal partnership does not exist. Do not rely on this for your partnership, as it may not suit you.

Pros

- More capital and other resources are available

Cons

- Liability: you are liable for your partners' acts as well as your own
- Formality: you should have a written partnership agreement laying everything out – pay, duties, capital, etc.; also taxation of partnerships can be quite complicated
- Limitation on number of partners in a partnership: twenty maximum (unless you are a partnership of accountants, solicitors, bankers, brokers, estate agents, architects, surveyors and the like)

Co-operative

Not a commonly used form of business enterprise – especially if profit and personal wealth creation is the main motivation. A co-operative is owned and controlled by all the people working within it (members). They are governed by the Industrial and Provident Societies Act 1965. The main feature of a co-operative is 'one person, one vote', which means they are unwieldy because decisions must be the consensus of the entire group. All workers must be offered membership as long as they meet the requirements of the co-operative. There is limited scope for rewarding individuals for contributing capital or working harder than other members.

Co-operatives can be registered, which will offer the members limited liability.

Pros

- Enables workers with a common objective to share resources to run a business enterprise
- Limited liability for members

Cons

- Formality: must register (unless all members lose limited liability) and submit annual accounts
- Unwieldiness: all decisions must be discussed and agreed by all members

Limited liability company

This is second only to sole-trader status in terms of popularity. There are in excess of a million businesses trading as limited liability companies. One of the main features of a limited liability company (usually referred to as a limited company) is that it has its own legal personality separate from its shareholders and employees (*Saloman v. Saloman*, 1897, established this principle). This means that if the business goes bust the shareholders have no further liability – they can lose no more than their investment (assuming they have paid the full amount for their shares).

All dealings are covered by Articles and Memorandum of Association, which state how both internal and external matters must be dealt with. Other features are that such an enterprise can raise additional funding by issuing further shares; must have at least two initial shareholders (one director and a company secretary); and must keep formal records and have accounts either audited or certified by an external accountant. Companies can be bought 'off the shelf' for under £200. Limited liability companies are governed by the various Companies Acts.

Pros

- Limited liability to members: cannot lose more than their initial investment

- Can raise additional funding by issuing more shares
- Cheap and easy to set up

Cons

- Formality: accounts must be prepared and subjected to external scrutiny. Must hold formal shareholders' meetings
- Directors may be liable to criminal prosecution for wrongful acts – can lead to fines and imprisonment

Authorised and issued share capital

Only limited companies can raise money by issuing shares. If your business plan shows that your business is likely to need additional cash funding in excess of £250,000, then issuing shares is the most common way of getting this level of funding. (We will look more specifically at funding in Chapter Six.)

The Memorandum of Association will declare the amount of share capital. For example, it may state that the company's share capital shall be £1,000 divided into 1,000 ordinary shares of £1 each. This is what is called the authorised share capital and its purpose is to specify the maximum number of shares that the company may issue without increasing its authorised share capital.

The company may actually issue less than the authorised share capital – in fact most do. Many off-the-shelf companies have an authorised share capital of £100 with an issued share capital of just £2 – with one share being held by each of the two founder directors/members.

If you are planning to raise, say, £2 million through a share issue then an authorised share capital of £100 is not going to be big enough. While shares do not have to be £1 shares, even if they were issued as 1p shares you would need an authorised and issued share capital of £20,000 to be able to issue 2 million shares. Shares do not have to be issued at par – in other words, you do not have to issue a £1 share for £1. In fact, shares are usually issued at a premium, e.g. a 1p share is issued for £1.

If your business is a limited company, you will need to state the authorised and issued share capitals and any plans you may have to issue additional shares to raise cash for the business. You must make sure that the authorised share capital is sufficient for your future needs. It is also common practice to state the main shareholders' names and their shareholdings.

Registered office, trading addresses, company registration number

The choice of business location is very important and will depend very much on where your customers are – it makes sense to be close to them. However, there are some areas where grants and lower wages and property rents make these attractive to set up or relocate a business. Wherever you trade from will be your main business address for administration purposes.

However, if your business is a limited company it will also have a registration number and must have a registered office – these are needed for more official communications. You are required to have a plaque with the company name and registration number outside the registered office. Quite frequently the trading address and registered office address will be the same. In this section you should include details of how the business can be contacted. This will include relevant telephone numbers, fax numbers and email and web addresses.

Professional advisers

Depending on why you are preparing your business plan it may be appropriate to have additional help from accountants, solicitors, stockbrokers, etc. Certainly, if you are trying to raise equity funding, then this help will be appropriate. If, however, you were just asking the bank for a small overdraft facility or requesting a lease from a landlord then this would be way over the top. In all cases you should include the name and address of the business's bank and any advisers you are using for this application.

2 Current mission and objectives

Without focus a business reduces its chances of success – there is every chance that it will pursue opportunities that are not right for it.

Case study

There is an apocryphal story about the chief executive of a large car-hire business that had made losses for several years. To get the business back on track he had cut out all the non-core business, which had included property. At last the business was now single-minded and profitable.

To help reinforce the new mission statement he had written a one-line sentence, which said something along these lines: 'We are in the business of hiring motor vehicles without drivers'. This mission statement was visible in most parts of the head office in London. One day, according to legend, this chief executive got into the lift from his office to go down to reception to be picked up by his chauffeur. 'Good morning, George,' he said to the lift man. 'It's a fine day today.' George replied, 'Yes, it is, sir. What are you going to do today?'

As the lift was descending from the fifteenth floor towards the ground floor he explained that he was going to have a look at a hotel which he was hoping to buy for the company. Immediately George the lift man hit the stop button, bringing the lift rapidly to a halt between floors, and took the lift back up towards the fifteenth floor, whence his boss had come.

'Why did you do that, George?' enquired the chief executive. George immediately responded, 'Sir, I'm taking you back to your office because I believe that you must be ill and need to rest. I'm assuming you must be ill because you've just told me that you're going to buy a hotel for our company. Surely, you must know that we're in the car-hire business, and that doesn't include buying and selling property.'

Even George, who was probably at the lowest level within the organisation, knew what business they were in – and especially what businesses they were not in. He was well focused.

Your mission statement should identify what you are trying to achieve now and in the short term – the current business. It needs to be very specific because this gives a clear indication to your employees, potential investors, customers and readers of your business plan. It has two main objectives:

- To rally the troops – get everyone pulling in the same direction
- To focus resources – to solve problems so that the business can move in the direction it wants to go

It should also explain:

- What business you are in and its purpose: e.g. 'We are in the car-hire business and we are trying to expand this business into the United Kingdom.'
- What your specific short-term goals are towards achieving this: e.g. 'Within the next two years we will establish a profitable car-hire business within London.'
- What your specific longer-term goals are towards achieving this: e.g. 'Within four years we will also have established a regional network.' (Objectives are covered in more detail in Chapter Three.)
- How you want to do business – your values: e.g. 'We will always respect our customers and value our staff.'

3 The management, key employees and organisation structure

As part of this 'stock take' of your current situation, you must include what is regarded as arguably the most important asset of any successful business – its people. You should remember that when banks, venture capitalists and so forth invest in a business they are primarily backing the management team to succeed. A well-respected colleague of mine was frequently asked what were the most important things he looked out for when he was looking to invest in a business. His answer was quite simple and always the same:

1 People
2 People
3 People
4 Product/service

He would always invest in people and if he believed in them he would then look at the product or service they were offering.

As part of your state-of-the-nation review you should detail your management team and key employees. Please do not make it like an Oscar ceremony's thank-you speech – the one where the recipient includes everyone from their parents right through to the tea boy on the set. You must be more selective.

The management team includes directors and the functional departmental heads (for instance, sales, production, marketing and finance) who are not directors. Under key employees you could include technical people or other individuals without whom the business would not be the success it is today (or hopes to be).

If yours is a small business it is of course likely that you do not have a management team and this exercise will highlight that. There is nothing wrong with that but you must recognise that an investor will notice this immediately and start to ask such questions as, 'What are you doing about succession planning?' or 'What happens if you are ill?' Or 'As you get bigger how will you manage with your limited management team?' Of course the answer could be, 'Yes, we recognise that and you will see that within this business plan we plan to recruit a general manager in six months' time and a finance director in twelve months' time.'

So what should you say about all these people? Well, include a very selective CV that is heavy on the current responsibilities and successes within this business, one that highlights skills, relevant qualifications and relevant past employment. If you are going to include it within the main body of your business plan, each person's CV should amount to no more than about a dozen lines. If it is going to be any longer than that, include the CV in the appendices and just include the briefest details within this section of the business plan.

Of course any team is only as good as the management structure it works in. What structure does your business have? If it is a small business it is likely to be flat or non-hierarchical – this means there are not many levels from the boss to the workforce. It may be that there are the directors or partners or just you at senior manager level with only foremen or supervisors between you and the workforce.

If, however, you are within a large, publicly owned business, then the chances are the organisation is very hierarchical. The structure could be: main board, subsidiary board, departmental heads, section heads, supervisors, workforce. Which is right for your business only you will know. Size will often dictate the type of organisation but complexity of business can also be a deciding factor.

I know a successful businessman who runs a multi-site business with 600 employees but has a very flat management structure with just two levels between him and the workforce. It works because he is very hands-on and his business is very straightforward.

You should be able to draw an organisation chart showing how your business is structured. The process of doing this will enable you to review how well it is managed. If your organisation chart shows that everyone seems to be reporting to you, it may be time to have another level of management so that you can be freed from more day-to-day matters to concentrate on the more strategic issues.

4 Milestones and financial performance to date

As a final part of your review of the business as it stands, you must include a potted financial history and the key historic milestones. Let's start with the milestones. In effect, this plots the business's history to date. It could include:

- When the business was started, by whom and where (front room, small factory, etc.)
- Why it was originally started and what markets and products it originally traded in
- Key milestones in terms of successes and failures – new products, new markets, changes of business direction, etc.
- Key milestones in terms of other events – new locations/factories, new ownership, large-scale additional equity/bank funding, number of employees, etc.

This will show the reader how the business has developed over time. All businesses need to change as they grow. If you can show that yours has changed successfully as demand has changed, then your reader will see this as a considerable strength. Of course it is possible that at this stage your business is so new that this section may comprise just one paragraph – don't worry.

Finally, you must set down some indisputable financial facts that show how your business has performed in recent years. There are two main reasons for doing this: (a) it shows your readers how your business has performed in the key areas of sales growth, profitability, financial strength and cash management; (b) it reminds you how well (or otherwise) your business has performed in these areas.

The most sensible way of providing this information is to have a financial summary in this section and copies of your last three years' audited accounts in the appendices. The financial summary is not supposed to be detailed – its purpose is to leave an impression (good or bad). The key figures to show are:

- Sales (last five years)
- Gross profit as a percentage of sales (last five years)

- Net profit (last five years)
- Net profit as a percentage of sales (last five years)
- Some key ratios (last five years), e.g. return on capital employed, gearing, interest cover, debtor days, stock days, added value per employee

All these areas are covered in more detail in Chapter Five – so don't worry if you're not too familiar with them now. However, they are important, since they help establish the financial shape that your business is in now prior to embarking on this business plan.

Chapter summary

In this chapter we have learned that:

- Your business plan should not be setting out a course that you have little or no chance of completing – recognise your strengths and play to them.
- There are many types of legal format that you can use for your business – some will be right for now and others may be required for the future as you grow and need more money.
- Missions and objectives are not business-school-speak. Missions are all about focus and objectives are the milestones on the way of getting where you want to go – make sure your business plan includes these.
- Your people and organisation are key to your success – who has been instrumental in delivering past success, and will you need more people for the future?
- You can't argue with numbers because they are the evidence of past performance – although they are the past they are also the future unless you do something to change the way your business performs. Make sure your business plan includes a summary of your recent financial performance.

CHAPTER FIVE

Let's look at some numbers

Chapter outline

There is an expectation that your business proposition will be profitable but that it may need additional funding. This is the place for you to show the scale and profitability of your business over the next twelve months, three years and five years. It will also show when you need cash and when you will be generating cash strongly enough to repay this. You will also need to have a keen eye for knowing when your business is marginal – break-even will help you here. This chapter tells you how to prepare these forecasts accurately and convincingly. By the end of this chapter you will have presented your financial case to your reader in the best possible way. This is the key section of your business plan.

Which parts of the business plan are covered in this chapter?

Section heading	What is covered in this section	Full business plan (external – raising money)	Full business plan (internal – performance enhancement)	Full business plan (internal – board approval)	Summary plan (external – lease, suppliers, etc.)
Financial forecasts	Profit and loss forecasts	Yes	Yes	Yes	Yes – but see comments below
	Cash flow forecasts	Yes	Yes	Yes	No
	Balance sheet forecasts	Yes	Yes	No	Yes – but see comments below
	Break-even analysis	Yes	Yes	Yes	No

Section heading	What is covered in this section	Full business plan (external – raising money)	Full business plan (internal – performance enhancement)	Full business plan (internal – board approval)	Summary plan (external – lease, suppliers, etc.)
	Key perform-ance ratios	Yes	Yes	Yes – but limited to profit and loss	No
	Assumptions	Yes	Yes	Yes	No
	Sensitivity analysis	Yes	Yes	Yes	No
Comments	This section shows the financial results that will result from your plan-ned actions.	Must be very comprehensive and not leave unanswered questions.	This must give full comfort that nothing has been overlooked.	Focus is very much on profitability and cash flow.	Information should be summarised and contained on one page.

Finance as a foreign language

I know that some readers may feel entirely comfortable with finance and producing financial forecasts. I am also aware that some of you may be preparing to run a mile just now. Don't. While this book does not pretend to be an accounting primer it will give you some basic guidance on how to prepare the financial information you will need to satisfy both yourself and your target audience. There is a real temp-tation for me to insert a short book on finance within this chapter – but I will resist. If as you read this chapter you feel uncomfortable then I make the following suggestions:

> ■ If you are sinking, get your accountant to help you. It may cost you – either a favour or hard cash. It will ensure that you get the job done right.
>
> ■ If you think you can do it but need a little help with a few concepts, try a good reference book. You can't go wrong with Frank Wood's *Business Accounting 1* and *2*.

There is no escaping preparing some financial projections – they are expected. They will help show how profitable (or otherwise) your business proposition is; how well it generates cash and when (and how much) additional funding may be needed; what you will spend both the business's and any investors' cash on.

Why we do the forecasting now

I know that some of you are thinking that it is heresy to do the financial projections now – before we have even looked at marketing, sales, production, people and so on. You may ask the question, 'How can I put in a sales figure when I haven't done any market research to tell me what I can achieve with my product or service?' Well, you are quite correct: you can't put in a sales figure that you can 100 per cent support – but you can start with an assumption and work from there. What if we sold £100,000 in Year 1, £120,000 in Year 2 and £150,000 in Year 3? What would profitability look like and how much cash would we need to achieve this?

I suggest that you start now to do the financial forecasts for the following reasons:

- You have already established some objectives – let's test these to see if they make any sense. Do these sales give the levels of profit that's required? Surely it is better to find out early on if your objectives are wrong, before you commit too much time to a business plan that is futile. I am suggesting that you do a 'what-if' profit forecast to demonstrate if at face value your objectives are achievable.

- If your initial conclusion is that at projected sales your profit objectives cannot be met, you can start to look at alternative strategies for profit enhancement. This might include improving the gross margin and/or reducing overhead costs.

- How does the cash flow look? It may be that, using your sales and profit objectives, you have severe cash-flow problems, which you may not have anticipated. This may cause you to revisit your objectives – especially if you know that additional funding is unlikely.

- How does the balance sheet look as the business is projected to grow? Why should you be interested in this? Because it will reflect any increasing asset base (fixed and current), show your ability to meet your short-term liabilities. It will highlight any vulnerability in your funding and enable you to review some key performance ratios, such as return on capital employed. Again this first 'what-if' may reveal that performance is too poor to attract the funding you require.

The end result of this first run-through of the profit, cash flow and balance sheet forecasts is that you should end up with something that prompts you to say to yourself, 'I like that – now how do we make that happen?' You can then focus the rest of the business plan on demonstrating how you can deliver. Alternatively, you may come up with profits and cash flows that you do not like and you may have to seriously rethink your business proposition. Either way, this initial exercise is invaluable.

A word of warning: this is what is known as the 'desired result' approach to forecasting; but it can also lead to what I call a spreadsheet exercise gone mad. You may recognise this – it's one where you pump in higher and higher sales figures, which churn out more profit and more cash. There is a very strong temptation to go too far – don't! Remember to subject these financial projections to a sanity test: you can't sell more than you can make, for instance, or, if you are accelerating production and sales, there are additional costs and cash requirements to go with them.

Remember, too, that your reader will also apply their own logic test to your forecasts and will soon spot unrealistic figures. You will find yourself having to answer questions like, 'I see gross profit increases from 40 per cent last year to 50 per cent in Year 1 of your projections, but I don't see how you plan to do this. Can you please explain this apparent miracle?'

Some basics before we start

Before we look at the financial forecasts it may be helpful to tell you about some important accounting principles and concepts.

Balance sheet forecast

This is a 'snapshot' of the business at a point in time (usually the financial year end) and shows 'where the business got its money from' and 'where the business spent this money'. That's it in simple terms, but we accountants have managed to make it more difficult by devising a language all of our own. The section of the balance sheet that shows where the business got its money from is called 'Financing' and is referred to as 'Liabilities' – because the business has acquired this money from outsiders. These outsiders are shareholders and providers of long-term debt and they provide (as their name suggests) long-term financing. On a short-term basis, a business can obtain financing from trade creditors, the taxman, the VAT man, etc. These are referred to as current liabilities.

The other side shows where the business spent this money, and these are referred to as assets – either fixed or current. Fixed assets are those that we buy solely so that we can carry out our business – land and buildings, plant and machinery, motor vehicles, etc. They stay in the business for a long time. Current assets are those that are constantly changing – stock, debtors, cash.

Of course this is a simplistic view of the balance sheet, but that's basically it. A few other things you should remember are that if your business is VAT-registered all the figures in the balance sheet exclude VAT, except for trade creditors and trade debtors. If your business is not VAT-registered the same applies but any assets that you have acquired are shown inclusive of any VAT.

Profit and loss forecast

This is often referred to as the 'moving picture' because it shows the measurement of profit (or loss) over a period of time (usually the financial year). If your business is VAT-registered all figures in the profit and loss forecast exclude VAT. However, if your business is not VAT-registered all your costs will include any VAT they had on them when you made the purchases.

Don't be confused by depreciation – it's a way of recognising that over time an asset is worth less than you paid for it. It's a charge against profits for using fixed assets. It is not setting aside cash for the replacement of your fixed assets. There are two main ways of calculating depreciation that you should be familiar with – straight line and reducing balance. The example below shows how both of these work:

	Straight line method	Reducing balance method
Original cost	£100	£100
Year 1 depreciation @25%	−£25	−£25
Written-down value (WDV)	£75	£75
Year 2 depreciation @ 25%	−£25	£18.75
(WDV)	£50	£56.25
Year 3 depreciation @ 25%	−£25	£14.06
(WDV)	£25	£42.19
Year 4 depreciation @ 25%	−£25	£10.55
(WDV)	£0	£31.64

As you can see, the straight line method writes the asset off in equal amounts – over four years in this example. The reducing balance method never actually writes off the asset and after four years some 30 per cent of its original value is still left on the books. Both methods are used but the reducing balance method is favoured by accountants. The actual rate of depreciation used depends on the type of assets and the useful life they are deemed to have.

As a quick aside, while depreciation affects your projected profit it has no effect on your taxable profit. The taxman adds back your depreciation to your net profit to arrive at taxable profit. In return he gives something called capital allowances – which may not be quite as generous as your depreciation.

You should be aware of some accounting concepts, which often cause the uninitiated a problem.

The realisation concept. Basically, this affects your sales income figure (top figure on your profit and loss forecast) and means this should be the value of goods dispatched and/or services provided to customers within the period in question. Note that this is not necessarily what you have been paid for.

The accrual concept. Basically, this means you match income and expenditure in the same period. There are cases in which this will affect your profit and loss forecast. Imagine you get your quarterly telephone bill at the beginning of July and this covers April, May and June – at the time you are preparing your June profit and loss. Would it be right to match the whole lot against June? No, it would not, because it should be matched against each of the months of April, May and June. The usual practice is to try to anticipate this situation and an estimate or accrual is made in each of the months of April, May and June – before you receive the actual invoice.

Cost of sales adjustment. Finally, watch out when calculating the cost of sales figure. It must (as its name implies) be the true cost of those sales made in that period. You must therefore adjust for any changes in stock and work in progress, which may affect your actual consumption of materials that have ended up in those sales made during the period. The example below shows how this is accounted for in the profit and loss forecast:

Sales		100,000
Material costs:		
Opening stock	25,000	
Purchases in period	50,000	
	75,000	
Less closing stock	60,000	
Cost of materials used		15,000
Direct labour		30,000
Cost of sales		45,000
Gross profit		55,000

Cash flow forecast

This is a unique statement, which shows only the flows of cash in and out of a business and the effect these have on the bank balance within the period. It is quite different from the profit forecast (although there are similarities in format) because it includes expenses, as they are paid (no attempt to match income and expenditure). All the figures include VAT where applicable (regardless of whether or not the business is VAT-registered). It also includes capital payments and receipts and payments of VAT, tax, national insurance, etc. Finally, it excludes depreciation (which should be in your profit and loss forecast) because this is a non-cash item.

How far ahead?

That concludes your accounting refresher, which hopefully makes you slightly better equipped to prepare your forecasts. The next key question is, 'How far in advance should you prepare your financial forecasts?' I know this sounds like a weasel answer but I always reply, 'As long as it takes to show the desired result.' And the desired result is: when the business returns to profit; when the desired level of profitability is shown; when cash flow becomes positive; when the overdraft is cleared; when the business demonstrates its ability to pay good dividends, etc.

As a general guide I would say your forecasts should cover one year for a lease application/tender document to a large PLC/internal use; three years for an overdraft facility; five years for a long-term-loan application or equity investment. Another question is, 'How much detail should I include?' Certainly for the first year you should include profit and loss figures and cash flow figures on a monthly basis. If after the end of the first year your business is either not profitable or not showing positive cash flow then the second year should also show figures on a monthly basis. Otherwise, I would suggest that you show any following years on a quarterly basis.

If you are a spreadsheet user then using one will greatly speed things up, especially if you want to carry out what-ifs. If you are creating your own spreadsheet (or even if someone else is doing it for you) please test-check some of the calculations. I have seen a case where the spreadsheet indicated an annual profit of £105,000, but, when the twelve months were added up, the real profit was only £55,000 – a bit of a shock! If you are not a whiz with spreadsheets get a colleague to help you, or go on a crash course and learn quickly. The skills you will need to create the forecasts used in this book are not immense – most basic spreadsheet users should be able to manage these.

At the back of this book you will find blank sheets to help you prepare all the forecasts you will need. You may find it helpful to copy these on a photocopier that has an enlarging facility and blow them up to A4 size. Ideally your forecasts should be printed and a spreadsheet will be best for achieving that. You can download all these spreadsheets free of charge from my website by accessing www.paulbarrow.co.uk. You can easily alter these spreadsheets, as they are all unprotected. All the spreadsheets are designed to print out in landscape mode on A4 paper. I hope this helps save you time.

Profit and loss forecasts

This has got to be the key forecast and as such is the logical place to start. In fact it is the only place to start since you need key information from the profit forecast to do the cash flow forecast. However as you prepare this forecast I want you to be thinking about break-even at the same time. Why? Because they share much of the same information and they are both key pieces of information. OK, so let's start to look at the key information you will include here:

Sales income

Eventually this will come from your detailed sales forecast (Chapter Eight) but first time through this might be based on last year's sales figure uplifted by some growth factor. It shows the value of goods or services you expect to sell during the year. Remember, whatever figure you put here you will also use for your break-even analysis later.

Cost of sales

Eventually this will come from your detailed production costs (Chapter Nine) but first time through this might be based on last year's figures. Don't forget that this is the cost of those goods sold in the period, so remember to make the stock adjustment (shown earlier in this chapter) to make sure you arrive at the right figure. In most businesses cost of sales will include materials and production/service delivery wages. Remember, whatever figure you put here you will also use for your break-even analysis later.

Gross profit

This is quite simply the difference between sales income and cost of sales. However, this figure is in my opinion the most important measure of performance in any business. It is a measure of the efficiency of the 'engine' of the business – your manufacturing/service provision. Your objective must be to maximise gross profit, aiming for gradual improvements each year. A slightly depressing observation is that after gross profit it's all spend, spend, spend – on expenses such as marketing, administration and financing.

Expenses

This is the collective name for every other business expense that is incurred in operating the business. It will include such things as rent, rates, insurance, advertising, salaries, depreciation and financing costs. Remember that you will use some of this information for your break-even analysis later.

Net profit

Finally, after all business expenses have been paid, the business has either made a profit or a loss, which we call net profit before tax. This is the difference between gross profit and total expenses. This is taxable at a rate dependent on the size of the net profits.

Cash flow forecasts

Having completed the profit and loss forecast, it is now time to focus on cash flow. Can I give you just a little insight into how a typical businessperson and bankers differ in their thoughts about profit and cash flow? A businessperson is usually very much in tune with their business's profitability – they understand gross profits, expenses and net profit pretty well. However, they really don't understand cash flow so well. They usually believe that their businesses are self-funding – even when they are growing quite rapidly. They don't like chasing their customers for payment – in fact they probably don't know how long it takes for their customers to pay them! This is why they generally have cash flow problems.

On the other hand, bankers are only too painfully aware of how businesses consume cash. Every day they see business bank statements that show payments constantly being made with very few deposits coming in from their customers. They know that every month is a cash flow crisis month – especially when the VAT is due for payment. They know that as some of these businesses grow the bank will be expected to provide the cash – even without being asked in many cases (because these businesses have not spotted the need for extra cash). The one thing they don't have very much of a handle on is the profitability of these businesses because a typical businessperson never tells them anything.

Cash flow is vitally important. Profitable businesses can go bust – not from lack of profit but from lack of cash. The purpose of the cash-flow forecast is to predict when you will need additional cash for your business and how much you will need. If you predict that your business will need additional funding in, say, two months' time, start to talk to your bank now. They will be more inclined to help you than if you leave it to the last minute and they start to bounce your cheques.

For those of you who don't yet believe that profit and cash flow are two different things, let me give you a very brief example. Geoff Podmore is an electrician and he has been offered two industrial contracts for a local builder. For these he will need to buy materials, use and pay subcontractors and give his customer credit while the work is continuing. Geoff has the following information:

	Job 1	Job 2
Sale value	£10,000	£20,000
Costs:		
Materials (paid cash)	£3,000	£6,000
Subcontract labour (paid cash)	£3,000	£6,000
Admin. expenses (paid cash)	£1,500	£1,500
Total costs	£7,500	£13,500
Profit	£2,500	£6,500
Start	beginning of Month 1	beginning of Month 2
End	end of Month 3	end of Month 6
Paid by customer	15 days after end of job	15 days after end of job

Geoff tells you that prior to commencing Job 1 he has £1,500 in his bank account. He also tells you that Job 2 is conditional on his finishing Job 1 first (and to his customer's satisfaction). At this point Geoff is very enthusiastic about these two jobs since over a period of six months he will make £9,000. But let's have a closer look at his projected profit and loss forecast and cash flow forecast to see how it all pans out. First let's look at Geoff's profit and loss forecast:

Geoff Podmore: profit and loss forecast

	Month 1	Month 2	Month 3	Month 4	Month 5	Month 6	Total for 6 months
Sales income			10,000			20,000	30,000
Less cost of sales		6,000				12,000	18,000
Gross profit			4,000			8,000	12,000
Expenses:							
Admin.	500	500	500	500	500	500	3,000
Total expenses	500	500	500	500	500	500	3,000
Net profit before tax	−500	−500	3,500	−500	−500	7,500	9,000
Tax							
Net profit after tax	−500	−500	3,500	−500	−500	7,500	9,000
Cumulative net profit after tax	−500	−1,000	2,500	2,000	1,500	9,000	

Remember that, even though each month he is spending money on materials and labour, there is no cost of sales in months 1, 2, 4 and 5 because there are no sales in these months. These costs go into work in progress. So far, so good – this looks reasonable. But how does the cash flow look?

Geoff Podmore: cash flow forecast

	Month 1	Month 2	Month 3	Month 4	Month 5	Month 6	Month 7
Inflow:							
Payment from customer				10,000			20,000
Total inflow				10,000			20,000
Outflow:							
Materials	1,000	1,000	1,000	2,000	2,000	2,000	
Labour	1,000	1,000	1,000	2,000	2,000	2,000	
Admin. expenses	500	500	500	500	500	500	
Total outflow	2,500	2,500	2,500	4,500	4,500	4,500	
Monthly movement	−2,500	−2,500	−2,500	5,500	−4,500	−4,500	20,000
Opening bank balance	1,500	−1,000	−3,500	6,000	−500	−5,000	−9,500
Closing bank balance	−1,000	−3,500	−6,000	−500	−5,000	−9,500	10,500

Ah! Suddenly it does not look anywhere near as attractive. In fact it looks as if Geoff will need to talk to the bank immediately to organise an overdraft of at least £9,500 to cover him for his cash shortfall. Of course, it all comes right in Month 7 – assuming his customer pays him on time. What is happening in Geoff's business is something that is euphemistically referred to as 'overtrading': his sales are growing (Job 1 £10,000 and then Job 2 £20,000) too rapidly for his cash flow to keep up. The reason his cash flow is under pressure is that he is funding the work in progress in each job (this would be highlighted in his projected balance sheet – had he done one) made up of materials and subcontract labour that he is paying cash for.

Balance sheet forecasts

Geoff's business was a good example of how an enterprise can get into trouble through rapid growth. The profit looked good but the cash flow was poor. It would be interesting to see how his balance sheet would have looked at the beginning, Quarter 1, and Quarter 2 and

Quarter 3, assuming he gets paid on time and does no other work. Let's assume that before he started Job 1 he had a van and equipment valued at £20,000. Don't forget that he also had £1,500 at the bank. All this had been funded by the £100 he originally invested to set up his limited company and £21,400 he had made in profits over the years. How would his balance sheets look?

Geoff Podmore:	balance sheet forecast			
	Opening balances	Qtr 1	Qtr 2	Qtr 3
Fixed assets				
<u>Cost</u>	20,000	20,000	20,000	20,000
Accum. depreciation				
Net book value	20,000	20,000	20,000	20,000
<u>Current assets</u>				
Stock and WIP				
Debtors		20,000	20,000	
Repayments				
Bank and cash	1,500			10,500
	1,500	10,000	20,000	10,500
<u>Current liabilities</u>				
Trade creditors				
Accruals				
Bank overdraft		6,000	9,500	
Short-term loans				
		6,000	9,500	
Net current assets	1,500	4,000	10,500	10,500
Net assets	21,500	24,000	30,500	30,500
<u>Financed by</u>				
Share capital	100	100	100	100
Reserves	21,400	23,900	30,400	30,400
	21,500	24,000	30,500	30,500
Long-term loans				
Capital employed	21,500	24,000	30,500	30,500

Now these help to tell us a bit more of the story about where the cash has gone and how this is not reflected in profit. Profits (look at

LET'S LOOK AT SOME NUMBERS

the reserves figure) are improving while net current assets are growing as a result of the debtor (Quarter 1 and Quarter 2) and bank overdraft, which is being used to fund the materials and subcontract labour (work in progress) as the job goes along (Quarter 1 and Quarter 2). Finally, in Quarter 3, it all comes good as the debtor is converted into cash – but note that net current assets do not change: debtors are converted to cash.

I do know from experience that most people have a real problem with balance sheet forecasts because (a) they don't fully understand them, and (b) they are difficult to do. However, they are important and if done properly they do impress bankers and other providers of finance. So how do you make sure you get your balance sheet forecast right? The key is keeping it simple and following common sense. Use the simple sheet that follows and keep to these suggestions:

> ■ **Fixed assets:** Don't forget to update for any purchases you plan to make and disposals of assets. At the same time don't forget to include in your cash flows. Don't forget to calculate depreciation and knock it off to arrive at the correct net book value (and profit in your profit and loss forecast).
>
> ■ **Current assets:** Now the fun begins. The key figures to get right are stock, debtors and the bank balance. Hopefully, the correct bank balance will come out of your cash flow forecast – but it probably will not first time round. Why not? Because it takes its base information from your profit and loss forecast, it ignores any build-up of stock and work in progress in your business as your enterprise grows. 'What do you mean?' I hear you ask. OK, it's time for another story.

Case study

A very good friend of mine, Andrew Waterfall, runs a fast-growing and exciting business called Improvision. Every year he produces a new business plan, which is most impressive in its detail. A long time ago when I was reviewing his five-year financial forecasts I noticed something quite strange in his balance sheet forecasts. I won't bore you with all the detail, but in essence it went something like this (these are not his figures):

Year 1: Sales: £1,500,000	Debtors: £150,000	Stock: £75,000
Year 2: Sales: £2,250,000	Debtors: £150,000	Stock: £75,000
Year 3: Sales: £3,000,000	Debtors: £150,000	Stock: £75,000

Year 4: Sales: £3,750,000	Debtors: £150,000	Stock: £75,000
Year 5: Sales: £4,500,000	Debtors: £150,000	Stock: £75,000

Well, have you spotted his deliberate mistake, because it was staring me in the face? Surely as his business grows, so will debtors and stock (and trade creditors, for that matter) – but this did not show that expected growth. Had he calculated debtor days and stock days (see later in this chapter) it would have highlighted this error. To my eye debtors look to be 10 per cent of sales and stock 5 per cent of sales. It seems reasonable to expect that as the business grows so will these and that unless they start to collect money faster or change their stock-holding policy these will also be 10 per cent and 5 per cent respectively of future sales.

Andrew listened to my suggestion and revisited his balance-sheet forecasts, which now looked like:

Year 1: Sales: £1,500,000	Debtors (10%): £150,000	Stock (5%): £75,000
Year 2: Sales: £2,250,000	Debtors (10%): £225,000	Stock (5%): £125,000
Year 3: Sales: £3,000,000	Debtors (10%): £300,000	Stock (5%): £150,000
Year 4: Sales: £3,750,000	Debtors (10%): £375,000	Stock (5%): £187,500
Year 5: Sales: £4,500,000	Debtors (10%): £450,000	Stock (5%): £225,000

Now this enabled Andrew to get his balance-sheet forecasts right but it posed another problem. By increasing debtors by £300,000 (£450,000 – £150,000) and stock by £150,000 (£225,000 – £75,000) over the five years it wiped £450,000 off his cash flow, which did cause a major headache. This growth in debtors and stock had a cash impact (it did not affect his profit and loss forecast) which he had overlooked. Remember that, as your business grows, debtors, stock and trade creditors will grow as well. This must be reflected in the balance sheet.

Now you know why I predicted that your original cash flow forecast may be wrong – it must take into account any growth in debtors, stock and trade creditors.

- **Current liabilities:** This should not be a problem as long as you follow the guide I gave you for current assets – apply the same principles.
- **Shareholders' funds:** This should be straightforward. Don't forget that if you are asking for any equity funding (i.e. money for shares) this should be shown here. Also, don't forget to include the increase in reserves as each period's profits are added to it.

> ■ **Long-term loans:** Finally you must update the long-term loans figure for any repayments you have made since the last balance sheet. It's OK because the figure you need for loan repayments should be in your cash flow forecast. Remember to take only the capital element off the figure in your balance sheet (the interest element is shown in the profit and loss forecast because it is a business expense).

I would of course be lying if I said preparing the balance-sheet forecast is easy. However, if you follow these guidelines you will do a reasonable job. Good luck.

Break-even analysis

At the same time as you were looking at profit I did invite you to think about break-even. You may remember that I said that some of the figures that you were using for the profit and loss forecast would come in useful for break-even. You will no doubt have heard of break-even analysis, but why is it so important? Using break-even you can plan to have a profitable business by focusing on the things that are important, such as margins, costs and profit. So how does it all work?

In any business there are inevitably costs – some that vary directly with sales (we call these variable costs) and those that you incur regardless of how much you sell (we call these fixed costs). Examples of variable costs are the material costs and direct labour that are used to make up the product or service that you sell – if you sell more units then these costs go up proportionately. At the same time we know that plenty of costs seem to be fixed regardless of how much we sell – rent, rates, insurance, heat and light, administration, salaries, depreciation. It's a bit depressing, really – we incur these fixed costs even if we sell nothing. Of course, against all these costs we do have something (hopefully) that will cover them: sales revenue. Now we start to have something quite useful that we can use to model how our business performs – it's called break-even analysis.

Let's use an example to help us. Alan Smith is planning to start up a business in domestic burglar alarms. He buys in ready-made alarm systems and uses a self-employed installer to fit them – he pays him a fee for each one he installs. He intends to employ a salesperson working on salary plus commission to get business for him. Below is his first-year profit forecast:

Profit and loss forecast for Year 1		
Sales revenue		£58,500
(450 units @ £130 each)		
Variable costs:		
Alarm systems	£20,700	
(450 units @ £46 each)		
Installation costs	£ 6,750	
(450 units @ £15 each)		
Salesperson's commission	£ 2,250	
(450 units @ £5 each)		
Sundry installation consumables	£ 2,250	
(450 units @ £5 each)		
Total variable costs		£31,950
(450 units @ £71 each)		
Gross margin		£26,550 (45.48%)
(450 units @ £130 − £71 each = £59)		
Fixed costs:		
Salesperson's basic commission	£ 6,000	
Salesperson's car	£ 2,500	
Office rent	£ 4,500	
Stationery and advertising	£ 7,550	
Total fixed costs		£20,550
Net profit		£ 6,000

This looks pretty much like a normal profit and loss forecast but the variable costs (which will be your cost of sales figure plus any other costs that you know are related to sales directly) are shown with a per unit value as well. The fixed costs will be the rest of your expenses (less those that you have already accounted for as variable costs).

So how do we calculate the break-even point for this business? 'OK,' I hear you asking, 'what's this break-even point all about?' It really is quite straightforward. Break-even point is that point at which sales revenue covers all costs exactly (variable costs and fixed costs). Let's look at the graph below to see this all illustrated:

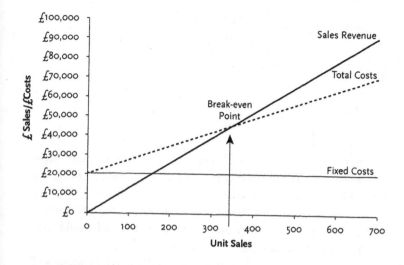

Looking at Alan's break-even graph we can see that, at somewhere around 350 units sold or about £45,000 of sales, his business's total costs are covered by his sales revenue. This is what we refer to as the break-even point. Looking at Alan's graph we can see that all sales below break-even (to the left of the break-even point) are unprofitable while those above (to the right of the break-even point) are profitable. In this particular case we are assuming that the maximum unit sales that Alan can make amount to 700 units. On this graph you can see that Alan's break-even point is at about the 50-per-cent-capacity mark, which is good. This leaves him plenty of capacity on which to make profit.

There is, however, a major limitation in using a graph to calculate break-even point. It is time-consuming (this one took me an hour to draw) and it's not very accurate. Using the same information we can calculate the break-even point mathematically.

$$\text{Break-even point} = \frac{\text{Fixed costs}}{\text{Selling price} - \text{unit variable cost}}$$

In Alan's case:

$$\text{Break-even point} = \frac{20{,}550}{(£130 - £71)} = 348.305 \text{ or } 348 \text{ units}$$

We can also arrive at the break-even point by using the formula below:

$$\text{Break-even point} = \frac{\text{Fixed costs}}{\text{Gross margin \%}}$$

In Alan's case:

$$\text{Break-even point} = \frac{20,550}{45.38\%} = £45,284$$

Those of you who do not believe that these are the same answer can work out that 348.305 units sold at £130 each = £45,279.65 (which is close enough for me).

So now we know what Alan has to sell to break even – 348 units or £45,284 in sales – but there are two more questions I would like to ask Alan about his business.

My first question is this: supposing he wanted to increase his profit from £6,000 to £10,000 in Year 1, what would his sales have to be?

To calculate this we use something called the break-even profit point. Basically it's the same as the break-even calculation except that we treat the new profit objective (£10,000) as an extra bit of fixed cost before we get to what we call the break-even profit point. The calculation is as follows:

$$\text{Break-even profit point} = \frac{\text{Fixed costs} + \text{profit objective}}{\text{Gross margin \%}}$$

In Alan's case:

$$\text{Break-even profit point} = \frac{£20,550 + £10,000}{45.38\%} = £67,320$$

So now we know that if Alan wants to make £10,000 profit in Year 1 he has to sell an additional £8,820 (£67,320 – £58,500). You can check this is right because £8,820 extra sales at 45.48 per cent gross margin gives him an additional £4,000 profit to add to the £6,000 he will already make.

The other question I might like to ask Alan is: how far can your sales drop below your target of 450 (his Year 1 forecast) before his business ceases to be profitable? This is what we call the margin of safety and it is calculated as follows:

$$\text{Margin of safety} = \frac{\text{Projected sales} - \text{break-even sales}}{\text{Projected sales}} \times 100$$

In Alan's case:

Projected sales £58,500 (450 units)
Break-even sales £45,284 (348 units)

$$\text{Margin of safety} = \frac{58,500 - 45,284}{58,500} \times 100 = 22.59\%$$

In summary, we can use break-even as both a predictive tool and an analytical tool. The margin of safety will come in particularly useful later on when we start to look at sensitivity and what to do if things don't go according to plan. However, it is now time for you to look at your business's break-even.

Key ratios

So far we have spent a lot of time looking at forecasts – profit and loss, cash flow, balance sheets, break-even. We need to provide the reader of your plan with some way of seeing at a glance how your business's performance stacks up. You may remember that I wrote earlier about a sanity test – this is part of it. We can use ratios to measure your business's performance by looking at:

- Trends: By comparing one year with another we can see what trends (good or bad) are developing in your business. For example, we could easily spot if gross profit has got better or worse over the three or five years that you are projecting – and ask the question, 'Why is it changing?'

- Comparing with similar businesses: Obviously yours is not the only business in the world in your marketplace, so why not compare it with other similar businesses. You can get this information from financial databases such as OneSource or FAME, which use information filed at Companies House. Your readers may have this information and will already be comparing your business with others they know of. You may then be asked questions such as, 'Why are your debtor days so much higher than the industry average?'

> To help you forecast: You may decide that your credit policy is to collect outstanding debts within 45 days, based on previous years' experience. You are then able to use this information in both the cash flow forecast and balance sheet forecast to improve their accuracy.

Ratios are calculated using key figures from both the profit and loss and balance sheets. While there are literally hundreds of ratios that could be used I will suggest that we use only a handful at this stage. Ratios are grouped according to what they focus on:

- **Measures of growth** tell us how key figures have changed over the years, e.g. sales growth.
- **Measures of profitability** tell us how good (or bad) the return has been for the key investors in the business, e.g. return on capital employed.
- **Measures of risk (or solvency)**, as the name implies, tell us how well funded the business is, e.g. gearing.
- **Measures of trading performance** – again, as the name implies – tell us how well the business is trading in terms of profitability, e.g. gross profit percentage.
- **Working capital (including liquidity and efficiency)** measures how well the business is managing its short-term assets and liabilities, a critical area, e.g. debtor days.

My suggestion would be that your key ratio summary could include some of each of these and that it should include the following:

1 **Sales growth percentage** – shows the year on year growth in sales, expressed as a percentage. Used to show the rate of sales growth for a business. Calculated as follows:

$$\frac{\text{This year's sales} - \text{last year's sales}}{\text{Last year's sales}} \times 100$$

2 **Return-on-capital-employed (ROCE) percentage** – shows the return earned on all the capital employed in the business (shareholders and long-term debt). This is a good measure of a business's ability to attract outside investment from all sources. Calculated as follows:

$$\frac{\text{Net profit before interest and tax}}{\text{Capital employed}} \times 100$$

3 **Gearing percentage** – shows how much of the long-term capital in the business has been provided by way of long-term debt and is expressed as a percentage. It is preferable for this to be less than 50 per cent to show that the business is not too dependent on borrowed money. Calculated as follows:

$$\frac{\text{Long-term loans (due after 12 months)}}{\text{Share capital + reserves + long-term loans}} \times 100$$

4 **Interest cover times** – shows the ability of the business to meet the interest payments out of profits expressed as a number of times, which is important in times of profit volatility. A value above 3 is preferred. Calculated as follows:

$$\frac{\text{Net profit before interest and tax}}{\text{All bank and loan interest}} \times 100$$

5 **Gross profit percentage** – the most critical profit performance measure of all, as it reflects the state of the 'engine' of the business. Calculated by deducting cost of sales from sales and expressing the resulting gross profit as a percentage of sales:

$$\frac{\text{Gross profit}}{\text{Sales}} \times 100$$

6 **Net profit after tax percentage** – shows the business's ability to generate sufficient profits to pay dividends and fund future growth. Calculated as follows:

$$\frac{\text{Net profit after tax}}{\text{Sales}} \times 100$$

7 **Current ratio** – measures the business's ability to meet its short-term liabilities on time using its short-term assets. This measure makes an assumption that all current assets can be realised at full value. Calculated as follows:

$$\frac{\text{Current assets}}{\text{Current liabilities}} : 1$$

8 **Quick ratio** – also known as the acid test. This is a more critical test of a business's ability to meet its short-term liabilities solely out of cash and debtors. It assumes that all other current

assets, particularly stock and work in progress, have no immediate value. It's what I call the 'when the creditors come knocking on the door, how do we pay them?' ratio. Calculated as follows:

$$\frac{\text{Debtors} + \text{bank balances} + \text{cash}}{\text{Current liabilities}} : 1$$

9 **Debtor days – also known as average collection period** and measures how well a business collects its debts, measured in days. This should be compared to a business's historic or stated terms to see how well it is performing. A key figure in projecting balance sheets. Calculated as follows:

$$\frac{\text{Debtors}}{\text{Sales}} \times 365$$

10 **Stock turn days** – measured in days to show how frequently stock is being sold and turned into profit. A key objective must be to keep stock for as short a time as possible. A key figure in projecting balance sheets. Calculated as follows:

$$\frac{\text{Stock (including work in progress)}}{\text{Cost of sales}} \times 365$$

11 **£ sales per £ of fixed assets** – I am a little reluctant to include this ratio because it does have some limitations, so I have modified it slightly to make it more useful. However, its purpose is to show how efficiently you acquire and use fixed assets within the business – if you are inefficient in your use a bank may decline to offer you additional funds to buy more! Calculated as follows:

$$\frac{\text{£ Sales}}{\text{Fixed assets @ original cost}}$$

This would conclude my list of key ratios that you should calculate from your profit and loss and balance sheet forecasts.

By now, apart from brain fatigue, you should have a pretty good picture of what the next few years of your business could look like in terms of profit, cash flow, balance sheet security and key performance ratios.

Assumptions

Of course, the job is only part done. To arrive at these financial projections you have made a whole series of assumptions, that you might just about remember, but your reader does not know about. Surely it would help them if they had the same knowledge – so go on, tell them all about the assumptions you have made in arriving at your profit and loss, cash flow and balance sheet forecasts. This will give them the chance to see if they agree with your assumptions and challenge them if necessary. Also, if you tell them now, it will save a lot of questions later such as 'I can't see in your cash flow forecast how long it takes for your debtors to pay you' or 'You say you are going to sell £100,000 worth of product in April – how have you arrived at this figure?'

This is not a massive section of the business plan – maybe just a page or two. However, it should pre-empt most of the picky little questions that nearly always get asked. I suggest that at least it should include statements covering the following:

Profit and loss forecast

A word of warning. Vague statements like 'We expect sales to grow by 10 per cent per annum' do not wash. Your business has no God-given right to growth – you must do something to achieve it. Everything that shows an improvement must be supported by some evidencing statement.

1 Sales: How these have been arrived at – could be based on last year plus a growth factor; could be based on some seasonal growth factors; could be based on a detailed sales forecast that follows (this is the correct answer and Chapter Eight covers this). Whatever you have done, tell the reader.

2 Gross profit: It is possible that you will be showing some improvement in this as the years go by. If you do, then tell the reader how you have arrived at the gross profit figures. An engineering business I know worked out the anticipated gross profit for every client and detailed these in its business plan.

3 Expenses: How have these been arrived at? Are they last year's figures uplifted for changes such as extra people, extra equipment, etc. Did you do a detailed recosting exercise – if you did, tell the reader and prove this with some details.

4   Interest and dividends: If your plan shows you are going to have to borrow money, do state how these loans have been treated in the profit and loss forecast. For example, you may make a statement such as, 'The business has assumed that it will receive a £100,000 bank loan repayable over 10 years at an interest rate of 10 per cent.' Fine. That tells the reader quite clearly how you have treated this loan. They may choose to disagree with whether they will give you the loan, but that's a different question. Also, if you are raising equity, you will need to state what your dividend policy will be. If you don't intend to pay any dividends in the first two years, say so.

Cash flow

1   Receipts from debtors: So when do your debtors pay you? What? Sixty days! Is this what you have put in your cash flow? Well no: actually, I put thirty days. Please be honest – both with yourself and with the reader. Don't cheat in your cash flow to get the funding down to a level that you know the bank will go to – because you are bound to fail to keep to this new overdraft level. Tell your reader exactly on what basis you have included receipts from debtors.

2   Payments to supplier: Exactly the same problem as with debtors. Do you have to pay up front for any supplies? If so state this here. Do you get offset arrangements where customers are also suppliers – quite common in some industries? Do you pay cash for anything to get better terms (naughty if this is contributing to the black economy)?

3   VAT: Don't forget to say if you are VAT-registered. You may be on quarterly or monthly returns – say which and include payments in the cash flow.

4   Tax: What assumption have you made about taxation in your profit forecast and when will it be paid in your cash flow?

Balance sheet

I think I have covered most of this earlier but please state all your assumptions about debtors, trade creditors, stock and work-in-progress levels. Also state what rates of depreciation you have used for any assets you have.

I hope you can see the value in this information because you will have used it in your forecasts.

Sensitivity analysis

You have done all these forecasts and I am now going to ask you to do them again. Well the truth is that the right forecasts are seldom the first ones that you do. Now you have done them once I want you to walk away from them – have a coffee or some other legal stimulant – and have another think about them. Ask yourself the question, 'What would happen if sales in Year 1 were 20 per cent less than I am forecasting?' There are loads of reasons why this might happen – some that you may already be aware of and others that you cannot predict. Revisit your forecasts to see the effects this will have on them.

If your business is still very healthy then congratulate yourself on having a robust business. However, the chances are that this will very significantly reduce both profits and cash flow. Quantify how much worse off your business will be under this scenario (or any other that you can think of) and state the effect. Do not provide several sets of complete forecasts for every scenario – this is confusing and the reader will discount the highest forecasts entirely in favour of the lowest. Stick with those forecasts that you believe are the most likely to happen and make a brief statement such as:

> We have arrived at our sales forecasts by reviewing our customers and their growth plans for next year. They have indicated that they would buy 30 per cent more product from us this year. If, however, they were to take 20 per cent less than forecast, our total sales would be reduced by £56,000. This would reduce our net profit by £10,000 after some other cost savings associated with not having this extra business, and would reduce our bank balance at the end of Year 1 from £105,000 to £97,000. We do not consider this position to be detrimental to the business's success.

Chapter summary

In this chapter we have learned how to:

- Understand the basics of how financial statements are produced.
- Prepare accurate profit and loss, cash flow and balance sheet forecasts for your business – make sure you have included these in your business plan.

Understand and use break-even analysis for your business – make sure you have included these in your business plan.

Use a series of key performance ratios to both check and act as a 'sanity test' on your business – make sure you have included these in your business plan.

Use sensitivity analysis to revisit your forecasts (as many times as you feel necessary) to see how well your business can stand up to uncertainty – make sure you have a paragraph in your business plan covering this.

CHAPTER SIX

But where will the money come from?

Chapter outline

Your cash flow forecasts have shown that you have got a big hole in your cash position at some time over the projected period. This is to be expected in most rapidly growing businesses, so don't panic. You do need to act now to find a suitable provider – don't wait until you run out of cash. But where should this money come from? That really depends on what you want it for. This chapter looks at the various ways of funding businesses – loans, grants, equity, etc. It will outline their differences and how they work. By the end of this chapter you will have identified how you can get outside money, how long it will take, what it will cost, etc.

Which parts of the business plan are covered in this chapter?

Section heading	What is covered in this section	Full business plan (external – raising money)	Full business plan (internal – performance enhancement)	Full business plan (internal – board approval)	Summary plan (external – lease, suppliers, etc.)
Funding required	Purpose	Yes	No	Yes	No
	Funding level required, timing and type of funding	Yes	No	Yes – but money will be provided by parent company	No
	The deal on offer/payback	Yes	No	Yes – but limited to payback	No

Section heading	What is covered in this section	Full business plan (external – raising money)	Full business plan (internal – performance enhancement)	Full business plan (internal – board approval)	Summary plan (external – lease, suppliers, etc.)
Comments	This section shows that you have thought through the funding proposition.	Must be very comprehensive and not leave unanswered questions.	Not required.	You have just got to convince the board that your proposition offers a better return than others they may be considering.	Tell them nothing – this is none of their concern, unless they ask.

Why do you need the money?

There are several possible scenarios that may come out of your forecasts. These could be summarised as follows:

1 Your business is very profitable, has good cash flow and is able to fund all projected growth comfortably. This is the perfect situation but recognise that it is one in a million and is likely to change at some time in the future. In the short term enjoy this golden period, manage the business well and use the cash surplus wisely.

2 Your business is profitable and has reasonable cash flow but is unable to fund an increased level of growth. This is a common situation and is what is known as a working capital requirement – best met by bank overdraft, assuming normal security levels are met.

3 Your business is profitable and has reasonable cash flow, but cannot fund necessary capital expenditure needed to progress the business. This is a one-off funding requirement and can be met by term loans, hire purchase, leasing or contract hire.

4 Your business is not profitable, has poor cash flow and is going through a prolonged period of recovery. This is again a working capital requirement and may in the short term be fundable by bank support – either overdraft or term loan – assuming normal security levels are met. However, there is a real possibility that this business is not fundable by normal bank

lending and is best supported by non-commercial funding, such as family, friends, grants, etc.

5   Your business is new and has the opportunity to have accelerated growth and very high profitability but because it has no track record has little cash and little security. To pursue this opportunity large amounts of cash are required for both cash flow and capital projects. This is not suited to bank funding because of the high element of risk and lack of security. It is well suited to equity funding.

The purpose of this is not to try to categorise your business and force it down a funding route, but to show you that there are many different ways of funding a business dependent on the need. It is possible that you are unaware of the variety of ways of funding a business and the particular characteristics each has. The starting point is to ask yourself some questions, the first one being, 'Why do I want the money?' To answer this you need to go back to your business plan to see what you are planning to do that needs funding. The example below is quite specific.

Beechwood Enterprises Limited needs to raise £250,000 which according to its business plan is needed to:

Buy fixed assets for Month 1 trading:	
Plant and machinery	150,000
Motor vehicles	30,000
	180,000
Provide working capital for the first 6 months	100,000
Total investment	280,000
Less investment available from business	(30,000)
Net funding required	250,000

This clearly tell me two things:

1   They know how much money they need and what they want it for.
2   They know when they want it.

You will need to be just as specific about your funding requirements in your business plan. Putting it simply you will need to do a shopping list – just like the one shown above.

Long-term funding

There is a truism that says you match funding to the need – in fact this was very clearly shown in the 'old-fashioned' style of balance sheet shown below:

Balance sheet @ 31/12/2000

Share capital	80,000	Fixed assets:	
Reserves	100,000	Land & buildings	110,000
Shareholders' funds	180,000	Plant & machinery	70,000
		Motor vehicles	20,000
Long-term loans	20,000		200,000
Current liabilities:		Current assets:	
Trade creditors	10,000	Debtors	20,000
Bank overdraft	20,000	Stock & WIP	10,000
	30,000		30,000
Total financing	230,000	Total assets	230,000

In this example we can see that long-term funding (shares, reserves and long-term debt) seem to have funded the long-term assets (fixed assets: land and buildings, plant and machinery and motor vehicles). Also we can see that short-term funding (trade creditors and bank overdraft) seem to have funded the short-term assets (debtors and stock and WIP). This area we call working capital has seen some change in the way it can be funded in recent years.

But nothing fundamentally has changed (apart from the way we present balance sheets) and this is how we should look at funding today.

Going back to our example Beechwood Enterprises Limited then, £180,000 of fixed assets could be funded by any of the following long-term funding methods:

Equity

The original founders of our example have bought shares in the business and left many years' worth of profits in the business to fund the fixed assets. This use of shares is known as equity funding and is particularly suited to raising large amounts. If you need to raise above, say, £250,000 then going outside the business to raise equity is an option. This can be done by going to a specialist equity provider, known as a venture capital provider. Below this level of funding it is not cost-effective to take this route – although there are some specialist equity providers who may be able to meet this need.

For sums up to around £100,000 a private equity deal could be arranged with, say, a business angel. These are high-wealth individuals who invest in businesses in which they can have some management involvement as well as a return on their investment. For very large funding then what is known as a public offering or placing is possible on either the Alternative Investment Market (AIM) or the Stock Exchange via a full listing. This is, of course, very time-consuming and costly, and does usually require a successful trading track record. Consequently, it is suitable only for raising millions of pounds.

Of course, this type of funding has a long-term cost to the business. These shareholders will want dividends for as long as they own their shares – which could be a lot longer than a bank loan. Also, dividends are not allowable against tax as a funding cost (unlike loan interest). Another point to be remembered when issuing shares is that your business must be valued so that a price can be worked out for the new shares being issued. This can be a contentious process with existing shareholders wanting as high a price as possible for 'diluting' their ownership of the business and potential buyers wanting as low a price as possible. Finally, remember that you have to be a limited company to issue shares. Sorry, sole traders and partnerships!

Debenture

While we are looking at sources of funding available only to limited companies we should also mention debentures. This is a bond, acknowledging a loan to the company, which bears a fixed rate of interest. This interest is payable regardless of whether profits are made or not (unlike dividends). The debenture can either be redeemable (at some future agreed date) or irredeemable, in which case redemption will take place only when the company is eventually liquidated.

To increase the level of security to the lender under a debenture, a charge may be granted over all or certain assets to a debenture holder. In the case of nonpayment of interest the debenture holder can seize these assets and dispose of them to pay the outstanding interest. This is known as a mortgage debenture, whereas those debentures that do not have this right are known as naked or simple debentures.

Commercial mortgage

This is the business equivalent of the type of mortgage that millions of people within the UK use to buy their homes. A commercial mortgage can be used to buy business premises but is normally repayable within between ten and fifteen years. Interest rates are usually fixed at the outset of the mortgage. The lender (usually a bank) has a first charge over the business premises being purchased. This means that in cases of non-payment of interest or capital the mortgagor (the lender) can call in the loan from the mortgagee (borrower), which generally means selling off the property to repay the loan. This type of loan is available to all types of businesses.

Short-term funding

In our Beechwood Enterprises example, the smaller fixed assets, such as motor vehicles, and current assets, such as debtors and stock, may also need funding. However, these require a shorter-term funding solution because their cycle of change is typically short-term – the motor vehicles every three to four years, and the stock and WIP on a constant cycle of change. In this example the motor vehicles have been funded by long-term debt – which is in this case hire purchase – and the stock and debtors are partly funded by overdraft. Let's have a look at the main options open for short-term funding.

Bank loan or overdraft

Probably the most common way of funding the majority of smaller UK businesses is a bank loan or overdraft. Obviously a bank loan is repayable over a fixed period and an overdraft is a continuous facility. It would, however, be wrong to think that an overdraft is not repayable. It is usually subject to an annual review and the bank has a right to ask for it to be repaid immediately if they wish. Bank loans and overdrafts are usually quite easy and quick to arrange.

Overdrafts have interest charged at a rate linked to the bank's base rate – typically between 1 and 5 per cent – which means, of course, that they can fluctuate in cost. There has been a tendency in recent years for banks to convert 'hard-core' overdrafts into medium-term loans (say three to five years) as a way of reducing a business's indebtedness. These short-term bank loans are typically used to fund small-assets purchases and the bank overdraft used to fund working capital (stock, debtors, etc.). Both these options are open to all types of business.

You may be interested to know that bank managers have come under pressure in recent years to improve the quality of their lending. They now manage their portfolios more closely and will try to keep what they regard as poorer deals off their books. Do not be surprised if they offer other means of funding, such as hire purchase, leasing, factoring, etc., which can be arranged by other associated businesses of their bank. This helps them to help you while keeping the risk off their books.

Hire purchase, leasing and contract hire

Hire purchase (HP), leasing and contract hire are ways of acquiring assets such as cars and equipment, when the business does not wish to (or cannot) use a bank overdraft or bank loan. Under an HP agreement the business is contracting to buy the asset over an agreed period of years. To this extent it is similar to a term loan, except that the rate of interest paid will usually be higher and there will be penalties for early repayment of the loan. At the end of the HP contract the asset belongs to the business.

Under a lease or contract hire the business is contracting to rent (not own) the asset over an agreed period of time – usually its useful life. It is responsible for maintaining the asset and returning it in good condition at the end of the period. There are penalties for early cancellation of the contract and at its end the asset will usually be required to be returned to its owner. An element of profit will be included in the rental cost so this will also cost more than a bank loan.

Under HP, leasing and contract hire a deposit is usually required and in some cases a final substantial payment may be required. Leases and contract-hire payments are subject to VAT and are allowable against the profit of the business. These are often referred to as 'off balance sheet financing' – because, since you are not buying the asset, they do not show on the balance sheet as either an asset or a liability. All these options are open to all types of business.

Asset based financing – factoring, invoice discounting and stock finance

Because the banks have been traditionally nervous about financing stock and debtors, new ways of financing these have emerged over the years. Asset based financing has emerged as a flexible way of providing working capital to fund growing numbers of debtors and amounts of stock using only these as security.

Factoring and invoice discounting are similar in effect and enable a business to access up to 80 per cent of the sales invoice value of the goods sold within 24 hours. This means that a business always has the level of funding it needs for the level of sales it is making. The balance is released (less financing costs) when the business's customer pays. This type of financing accounts for an increasing proportion of the funding of UK working capital and has shaken off the earlier stigma it seemed to have. Most banks have an associated business offering these services. What's the difference between the two?

- **Factoring:** The business sells its invoices to a factor and contracts its sales ledger administration and debt collection to the factor. This can include full bad-debt protection (non-recourse factoring) or exclude bad-debt cover (recourse factoring). This is usually applicable to businesses projecting turnover in excess of around £100,000 per annum. Obviously, this level of service has a higher cost than just financing the cost of the money advanced.

- **Invoice discounting:** The business exchanges sales invoices for cash but retains full control over its invoicing and debt collection. Bad-debt protection can be provided. This will usually be the cheaper form of debtor financing if no other service is being offered. This is usually applicable to businesses projecting turnover in excess of £750,000 per annum.

Stock finance is quite a recent innovation, created through need. The stock itself is not funded but is used in conjunction with either factoring or invoice discounting to make up to 100 per cent of the sales invoice value available almost immediately. In effect it is an additional security for the lender. This combination of stock finance and factoring/invoice discounting is offered by the specialist banks and is not generally offered by the high street variety.

Note that the use of any of the above will reduce a business's bank overdraft facility (if it has one) because the usual security for an overdraft (debtors and stock) has been given to the specialist lender.

Letters of credit

If your business buys in goods from abroad then an additional complication frequently arises. Overseas suppliers almost always require payment before the goods are shipped. Of course, as the buyer of these goods, you will almost certainly be reluctant to pay for them before you have received them. An additional cash flow problem will arise because you will be paying for them some months before you will have sold them and consequently will not have been paid by your customer. Letters of credit (LC) are the internationally recognised way of ensuring that the overseas supplier has his guarantee of payment at the agreed time conditional on the goods being shipped.

This guarantee (LC) will be provided by your bank and will therefore come out of any overdraft facility that you may already have – not be in addition to it. Your overseas customer can then use the LC to borrow against or as an assurance that your bank will guarantee payment to his bank. Your bank will charge a fee depending on the amount being guaranteed.

Small Firms Loan Guarantee Scheme

I know that we have already covered bank loans earlier but a major problem that prevents many small businesses from getting a loan is security – or, more correctly, lack of it. A loan is arranged with a bank in the traditional way but is arranged under this scheme, which means that the Department of Trade and Industry (DTI) guarantee it. It is specifically available to most small and medium-sized businesses that have a viable business proposition but do not have adequate security to get bank funding. It is available for loans from £5,000 to £250,000 over periods of two to ten years and for most business purposes. The DTI will guarantee to pay the lending bank up to 85 per cent of the outstanding loan if the borrower fails to repay. However, this type of loan cannot be used to repay existing funding: it is to be used only for additional funding.

Arrangement fees are payable and a premium on the guaranteed part of the loan is payable to the DTI. The high street banks administer this scheme – so approach your bank. Obviously you will need to put forward your case (this business plan will help) and convince your bank. Loans up to £30,000 can be authorised immediately by the bank – above that, a second, independent, manager within the bank will need to authorise the deal and it will be sent to the DTI for approval (usually rubber-stamping). Available for all types of business and is something that you should seriously consider as part of your funding strategy.

Grants and awards

Your business may be located in a region that has been identified for special support. Regional Selective Assistance (RSA) is aimed at giving discretionary grants to businesses that want to relocate or expand in these areas for projects that create new jobs or protect existing ones. There are several examples of this. REGs (Regional Enterprise Grants) to smaller businesses to support capital projects up to 15 per cent of the costs (up to a limit of £15,000) are available. The Rural Development Commission (RDC) may be able to give grants to convert redundant buildings. In addition 'soft' loans are available under the Small Firms Training Loan scheme and Career Development Loans scheme.

Other support is aimed specifically at businesses involved in innovation and technology. These awards are not dependent on geographical location. Examples of these are:

- SMART Award, which is worth up to £45,000 for businesses with up to fifty employees to support innovative technology.
- SPUR Award, which is worth up to ECU 200,000 for businesses with up to 250 employees to support significant technology advance.
- TCS (Teaching Company Scheme), which will help most small businesses obtain the use of a graduate for up to two years for about 30 per cent of the real cost.

A business can apply for all these grants – they are not mutually exclusive. My friend Andrew Waterfall, who runs Improvision, has had all of these. Again, a business plan is required and you must remember that these are effectively competitions because there is a limited pot of money to be awarded. Remember:

- Most grants are awarded throughout the year: so there are generally no cut-off dates for applications – unless a grant is coming to an end. Most grants are specifically targeted to alleviate unemployment and are available to businesses in designated geographical areas.
- Some awards are annual competitions, so there are cut-off dates for applications. Some may be held once or more than once a year. In some cases there are various stages to the competitions. However, to be successful, your business must be highly innovative and technology-based.

In summary, there are a wide range of funding options for both long- and short-term needs – in fact the array of options can be quite bewildering. Do look carefully at each of these options to see if they may be appropriate to your needs. If you need to find out more about any of these look in the appendices for contact details – but be aware that grants and awards come in and out of favour, so check to see if the one you're interested in is still available.

When do you need the money?

Hopefully, by now, you have established how much money you need. You may also have started to narrow down the possible sources of this money. The next question to answer is, 'When do I need this money?' Your business plan must state quite clearly when you will need the various cash injections. Fortunately, in most cases, it is not all at once.

If we go back to our Beechwood Enterprises example, we know that they need £250,000 of additional funding – but do they need it all at once? Well, it is likely that the £150,000 for the plant and machinery may be needed earlier than indicated if it is to be ready for use in Month 1. However, the £30,000 for motor vehicles will have to be paid only when they are delivered, which will be in Month 1. Finally, the working capital will be needed at various stages over the next six months only and will in all probability peak early on and reduce in the later months (of course a cash flow forecast would show this quite clearly). It would now be possible for the business to set down when it needs the money and how much (as well as why, which we covered earlier). The business can now complete the final part of its funding statement in its business plan:

Having identified how much funding is required and for what purpose (see earlier section) the business (Beechwood Enterprises Limited) proposes to raise the £250,000 as follows:

1. An equity investment of £150,000 will be made by two business angels in Month 9 (previous financial year) and this will be used to acquire the plant and machinery in Month 10 (previous financial year). This will ensure that it is fully operational for Month 1 production. At this stage we have a written commitment to these funds subject to final details on the company valuation [see later on valuing a business] and a written statement from the business on dividend policy.

2 A bank overdraft facility of £130,000 is required to fund working capital requirements over the first six months. The cash flow does indicate a requirement of only £100,000 but the management believes it is prudent to allow a little headroom in case there is any unforeseen slippage during this period.

3 The financing of the £30,000 motor vehicles (two sprinter vans) is being provided by Mercedes Benz finance by way of contract hire over 36 months. This agreement has been signed and approved for delivery of the vehicles in Month 1. This will require an up-front payment of £3,000 to cover the first three months' payments, which the business will pay out of its own funds.

4 We have in reserve £27,000 of cash, which will serve as a contingency for unforeseen working capital requirements.

Clearly, if your business needs to arrange additional external funding it has got to provide an attractive proposition. Hopefully, your business plan will provide the evidence that persuades an outsider to part with their money. However, you will have to provide some other statements that convince them – this is where you do it. What you say is entirely dependent on whom you plan to get the money from.

Paying back the loans

External loans

As already mentioned, arranging most loans is relatively straightforward. The banks will have standard forms, which will focus on the business case (which your business plan will justify) and security (which your forecast balance sheets will also justify). I would suggest that your plan includes a brief statement confirming:

- How much you want to borrow
- Period of loan
- Assumed rate of interest
- Monthly capital and interest amounts you have included in your forecasts
- Calculation of gearing and interest cover after the loan – to convince the bank that it does not significantly breach the 50 per cent rule and that you can afford the interest payments

Internal loans

If your business plan is being used internally to divert funds to your business or business unit, then a slightly different approach will be used. The main board, or whoever is going to provide the funding, will not have a bottomless pit of money. They will be looking to invest in projects that have the best payback. Consequently they will want to find some way of comparing a whole range of projects, including yours. How can this be achieved?

Payback period

This approach shows how long it will take to repay the investment, usually in months or years. A simple example will help explain this. A business wants to borrow £10,000 to fund a project. According to its projections it will make profits of:

Year 1 profits	£4,000
Year 2 profits	£5,000
Year 3 profits	£6,000
Year 4 (last year of project)	£2,000
Total	£17,000

Looking at this example we can see that payback does not quite occur in Year 2 because the cumulative profits of £9,000 (£4,000 + £5,000) are not greater than the £10,000 invested. It does in fact happen before the end of Year 3 because by then it will have made cumulative profits of £15,000 (£4,000 + £5,000 + £6,000). Assuming that profits accrue evenly during Year 3 we can calculate that each month it makes £500 profit (£6,000/12). So, by Month 2 in Year 2, it has made the extra £1,000 profit that when added to the cumulative profits for up to Year 2 (£9,000) gives the £10,000 profit to equal the investment made. So in this case payback is two years and two months.

Overall return

Another approach that might be used is to look at how many times they will get their original investment back over the period of the investment. In the previous example after four years the business has made a total return of £17,000, so the overall return is 1.7 times (£17,000/£10,000).

Discounted cash flow (DCF)

This approach takes the net cash flows for each year and uses a discount factor to reduce to present-day values the value of cash flows in future years. If you want to find out more on DCF I suggest that you have a look at *Business Accounting 2* by Frank Wood.

Your project can now be compared with other projects that may be competing for the same funds. The decision may be taken that, while a payback period of two years and two months is attractive, an overall return of just 1.7 times in four years is not good enough.

Equity investment

Finding and securing an equity deal is quite a different matter. It is hardly ever straightforward so perhaps a little guidance may not go amiss.

Finding a partner

Let's start with the most difficult first: how do you present the right deal to get all the money without giving up too much equity? Another question you may ask is: how long does it usually take to raise money this way – and does it cost a lot? OK, let's start at the beginning. In our example, Beechwood Enterprises Limited had found a couple of business angels who wanted to invest. But how did they know where to look in the first place to find a potential investor? There is an excellent source of information that I can point you to: the BVCA (British Venture Capital Association) (see appendix for contact details) has lots of help and guides, which are mostly free. However, I would like to point out the following publications that will help you find a suitable equity partner:

> ■ BVCA, *Sources of Business Angel Capital* – which tells you how to find a business angel network and how the process works. It gives a profile on each of the networks; how much they typically invest and what type of industries they like to invest in; and full contact details.
>
> ■ BVCA, *A Guide to Venture Capital* and *Directory of the UK Venture Capital Industry* – the first publication explains in layman's terms the venture capital process and how to produce a business plan, and the second gives a detailed list of all the venture capital providers in the UK together with their investment preferences.

Hopefully, guides like these and the help of your local business link will help you to find an appropriate funding partner. Remember, unlike banks, which are pretty much the same (they will hate me for saying this), venture capital providers are quite different from each other. For example 3i PLC are the biggest of the UK providers of venture capital and have provided approximately £10 billion to businesses of all sizes in all industry sectors and at every stage of development. However, in contrast, Seed Capital Limited have provided about £3 million to mostly innovative start-up businesses.

The next stage is the 'beauty parade', where you and your management team appear before the potential investor. Here they size you up to see how you tick, your motivation, your commitment, and try to pick holes in your business plan. Assuming you get through this stage you will start to enter into the negotiations before completing the deal. Let's have a quick look at valuing your stage.

Valuing your business

Let me say something up front. While valuing a business is a well-trodden process there will be times when a business will be worth more (or less) than the underlying financial projections. This may be due to the venture capitalist or business angel wanting to do the deal with you because they want your type of business in their portfolio. On the other hand, if they have already invested in too many businesses like yours (sector/size) that year they will try to give you such a rotten deal as to drive you away.

Of course, I can't give away all my valuation secrets – otherwise I will get thrown out of the magic circle. However I can tell you the basic rules, which are incredibly simple. Assuming that the investor is interested in your business, then the following are the key factors taken into account in valuing your business:

1 **The perceived risk:** If yours is a new business with no track record, unproven management and a new product/service then this will attract a high-risk rating. On the other hand, if your business and management have a track record and the product/service is already recognised (you are just doing it better/cheaper/faster), then this will be seen as having very little risk. This factor may be used to adjust the required rate of return or downgrade the future value of your business.

2 **Your customer base:** If your business plan shows a good

spread of customers with none accounting for, say, more than 10 per cent of your sales, then this will be favoured. On the other hand, if your business has a small customer base it will be seen as very vulnerable and this will concern your investor. This factor may be used to adjust the required rate of return or downgrade the future value of your business.

3 **Maintainable profits:** This is key to the valuation of your business. An investor will value your business on what he believes your future maintainable post-tax profits will be. Of course, it is quite likely that your Year 3 profits are projected to be higher than those of Year 1 – that's OK, but your investor will discount profit forecasts further than one year ahead so it may not be advantageous to base a valuation on, say, Year 4 profit forecasts.

4 **Required rate of return:** This will obviously affect valuation. Let's say that a risk-free investment (e.g. building society) is yielding 5 per cent. An investor may want 20 per cent per year, which equates to 2.5 times their investment in five years, for a low-risk investment (as measured by 1–3 above). On the other hand, this same investor may want 40 per cent per year, which equates to 5.4 times their investment in five years, for a higher-risk investment. You may think this is greedy but if they make higher-risk investments then the chances are that out of, say, every ten investments six will bust – so the remaining four have to make a higher return to get an acceptable overall result.

5 **Industry Price/Earnings (P/E) ratio:** The final consideration must be how many years' worth of profits the investor is paying for to arrive at the future value for the business. If you have, say, an engineering business making £50,000 per annum (and capable of making it for many more years) would you be prepared to sell it for £50,000 (one year's worth of earnings)? Of course not. So how many years' worth of profits should an investor pay for?

For more traditional business where maximum profitability is being achieved now (such as engineering) the P/E ratio (or profit multiple) is likely to be low – say three to six times. That means that an investor will pay three to six times the annual maintainable profits to arrive at the future value of this business.

On the other hand, where the business is in a new and innovative sector (the Internet-based businesses are a good example of this) in which maximum profitability is not being achieved, the P/E ratio may be as high as twenty or thirty times – because the investor is expecting better to come.

The choice of P/E ratio will have a profound effect on the future value of the business. It is not correct to look in the *Financial Times* and take an average P/E from there because these businesses are quoted (therefore have a larger market for the shares) and bigger (therefore a lower risk). The correct approach is to look for similar businesses that have sold recently – this may come from talking to an experienced intermediary – and adopting a similar P/E.

The final part of the equation, which does not affect the valuation, but does affect how much equity an investor will receive, is the amount of money you need. For example, if your business is valued at £150,000 and you want £50,000, an investor will get 33.33 per cent of the equity (50,000/150,000).

OK, let's look at an example to see how it could all work out in practice. Beechwood Enterprises Limited has been trading for one year as metal finishers with an inexperienced management team. To fund its next stage of growth it has decided to raise £150,000 by means of an equity investment. Its projections are as shown below:

	Turnover	Profit after tax
Current year	£375,000	£37,500
Year 1	£500,000	£62,500
Year 2	£662,000	£75,000
Year 3	£850,000	£112,500

Let's assume that a P/E ratio of six times has been agreed and that the investor is looking for a 35 per cent return because they perceive the business to be quite high-risk. How, then, should we value this business?

Stage 1: What is the future value (FV) of the business?
Using the formula: FV = maintainable profits × P/E value

Year 1   Profit £62,500 × 6 (P/E)   = £375,000 future value
Year 2   Profit £75,000 × 6 (P/E)   = £450,000 future value
Year 3   Profit £112,500 × 6 (P/E) = £675,000 future value

On the face of things it looks straightforward – we should choose the year that yields the highest value, which is Year 3 profits. Well, because this is two years away, our investor will discount this by 35 per cent for each year away. So let's look at these three years again, applying this factor and using the following formula:

$$\text{Present value (PV)} = \frac{\text{Future value (FV)}}{(1 + i)^n}$$

Where: i = Investor's required rate of return
        n = Number of years until forecast profits

$$\text{Year 1: PV} = \frac{375,000}{(1 + 0.35)^1} = \frac{375,000}{1.35} = £277,777$$

$$\text{Year 2: PV} = \frac{450,000}{(1 + 0.35)^2} = \frac{450,000}{1.8225} = £246,913$$

$$\text{Year 3: PV} = \frac{675,000}{(1 + 0.35)^3} = \frac{675,000}{2.460375} = £274,348$$

On this basis it clearly makes sense to use Year 1 forecast profits because this yields a present value of £277,777. The other years yield lower present value because of the discount factor being used.

Stage 2: How much equity will the investor acquire?

The final stage is quite straightforward and calculates how much equity they will get for their £150,000. Having established that the business is worth £277,777, then £150,000 buys 150,000/277,777 = 54 per cent of the equity.

Of course this calculation is based on the investor accepting the management team's forecasts at face value, which, of course, they may not: they may want to reduce these figures.

Negotiating and completing the deal

Let me tell you now that deals are not done overnight and the more you want, the longer it can take and the more it will cost you. For example, if you wanted £100,000, then this would be within the scope of a business angel to provide. This is a fairly informal process and does not need a lawyer. If the investment was being provided by a single investor a good accountant could do the whole process within a few hours of his time and within, say, a month of elapsed time. The arrangement costs could be a few hundred pounds.

On the other hand, if you were raising, say, £750,000 via a venture capital provider the process is both longer and more expensive. Lawyers and accountants will be involved on both sides. A process called 'due diligence' will be gone through – this is where the team putting forward the business plan guarantee that they are not telling porkies. Such a deal might take three months to complete and have costs of £50,000 for the various advisers, etc.

Always remember that everything is negotiable and, if you feel strongly about something, stick to your guns. If you are raising a large sum of money via venture capital there will be a subscription agreement or similar lengthy legal tome. This lays out the rules of the game. It will include things like:

- What package you and your senior management team can have: this means salary, cars, other perks. Don't short-change yourself. If you are currently underpaid don't spend the next few years like this – it does not suit an investor to have you demotivated. Stick out for what you believe is right.

- How you can run the business: this means what authorisation is required and when. For example, an investor will attempt to restrict your ability to spend money without his authority: for instance, capital projects above £5,000 may need authority; unplanned revenue items above £1,000 may need authority. If these will effectively tie your hands and stop you from managing the business, tell them and get reasonable limits set.

- Day-to-day running of the business: The key figures from your business plan will be embodied in the agreement. If you do according to plan all will be sweetness and light. If you do worse all manner of nasties may descend on you. Read carefully what these may be and do not agree with them if they seem unfair. For example, the investor may try to impose a non-executive chairperson on you if profits are not up to par – resist.

- Non-executive directors and reporting: This is the investor's way of interfering in/influencing your business. You must, of course, understand their position. If they have just given you £500,000 they don't want to lose it, so they want to take out a little extra insurance. It may be that a non-executive finance director is a great idea – in that case, grab it with both arms if it does not cost too much. If the non-executive is going to cost a lot, you must question the value for money – how much and how many days a month do I get? If they want quarterly accounts then I would say that is reasonable. If they want monthly accounts, question why, and kick if you don't like it.

> The Ratchet: This is the way venture capitalists like to incentivise senior managers in the business. Basically, it is a way of giving you more shares for above business plan performance. The rationale is quite straightforward. If you can make the business more profitable it will be worth more when it comes to disposing of it. If you can do that you will make them richer, so they are prepared to give a bit of this extra profit back to you – not as cash but as shares. You can negotiate the detail of the ratchet.

There will be other areas for negotiation such as service contracts, tie-ins, etc. Remember: everything is negotiable – they may be just trying it on.

Exit routes for your investor

Your investor will be looking for an exit route right from the start – they are not to be regarded as a partner for life. They will mostly be looking at a time scale of three to seven years for their investment. After this time they will want to sell their shares on to someone else at a handsome profit. In fact they will want you to help them in this process when the time comes. So what are the likely exit routes for an investor?

> Trade sale: The most common exit route is to sell the business on to another business – usually in the same industry (or complementary) and frequently a larger competitor. This can be a fairly quick process but generally yields a lower price than a public offering. However, if the business is not profitable (or has underperformed) this is frequently the only exit route.
>
> Public share offering: The dream of many people is to float their business on either the full stock market or the alternative investment market (AIM). You do not have to sell all your equity – just sufficient to buy out your previous investor. This route usually gets the best price – but only if your business is very profitable (established business) or can demonstrate potential profit (new business). However, this is by far and away the least likely exit route.
>
> Share repurchase: This is an exit route for seriously underperforming businesses, whereby the management team buy back their own company at a discount. In effect the investor 'wants out' and is prepared to cut their losses. If the business has performed to plan the buy-back price would usually be too high for the management to fund.

Your plan should state the deal that you are offering a prospective equity investor in terms of the percentage equity they will get and any future dividend policy. In Beechwood Enterprises Limited they stated:

> In return for an equity investment of £180,000 we will offer the investor(s) up to 54 per cent of the ordinary shares of the company. Our dividend policy will be:
>
> | | |
> |---|---|
> | Year 1: | No dividend payment |
> | Year 2: | Dividend payment: 5% of post-tax profits above £150,000 |
> | Year 3: | Dividend payment: 7% of post-tax profits above £200,000 |
> | Year 4 onwards: | Dividend payment: 10% of post-tax profits above £250,000 |
>
> It is anticipated that by Year 5 the business will have achieved sufficient size and profitability to be disposed of to a third party. It is our intention to find a trade buyer to acquire the whole business at an appropriate time and price after this point. This would be subject to full consultation and agreement of all the major equity partners.

Chapter summary

In this chapter we have learned how to:

- Tell a possible lender/investor how much money we need; what we need it for; when we need it; and what's in it for them if they provide it.

- Recognise that there are numerous different sources of money for both long-term and short-term needs – show in your business plan which ones you want to use.

- Understand how each of these possible funding methods works and whether they will work for you.

- How to value your business if you need to raise equity funding.

- Negotiate a good deal if you are looking to attract an equity investor.

CHAPTER SEVEN

What about some market research?

Chapter outline

Unless you understand your customers and their needs you will not sell a thing. So how do you find out about them? It's market research – and there's tons of information available to help you. Who else wants your customers? Your competitors. Who are they, where are they and where is the chink in their armour? Find this out and you can beat them. Now you know all about your customers, how do you prepare a meaningful sales forecast? This chapter tells you how to carry out your market research, analyse your customer needs and identify and defeat your competitors. By the end of this chapter you will have identified where your customers are coming from and will be able to prepare your sales forecast.

Which parts of the business plan are covered in this chapter?

Section heading	What's covered in this section	Full business plan (external – raising money)	Full business plan (internal – performance enhancement)	Full business plan (internal – board approval)	Summary plan (external – lease, suppliers, etc.)
Markets and competition	Market trends and projections	Yes	Yes	No	No
	Sales forecast	Yes	Yes	Yes	No
	Current and proposed customers	Yes	Yes	No	No
	Competitor analysis	Yes	Yes	No	No

Section heading	What's covered in this section	Full business plan (external – raising money)	Full business plan (internal – performance enhancement)	Full business plan (internal – board approval)	Summary plan (external – lease, suppliers, etc.)
Comments	This section shows the ammunition you have to support your financial projections. It shows that there is a marketplace and that you can sell what you are forecasting.	Must be very comprehensive and not leave unanswered questions.	Must be very comprehensive and not leave unanswered questions.	They already know your business, so limit the detail.	Tell them nothing – this is none of their concern, unless they ask.

Why you need to know about customers and competitors

I may have misled you slightly in Chapter Five if I implied that the financial projections were the biggest part of your business plan – they are the icing on the cake, assuming that the rest of the cake is up to scratch. Knowing about your customers and competitors is key to your business success. Whoever reads your business plan needs to be convinced that you have done your homework, amassed the evidence and put forward a convincing argument.

I cannot stress the importance of this section too much. Without sound marketing information your business proposition is without foundation and your financial projections will be seen to be just supposition. It will be even worse if yours is a new business: there is no history, so how is the reader to be believe your sales figures in your forecasts? My experience of reviewing business plans is that at least 70 per cent have an unconvincing marketing section.

You may remember that earlier I told you about three guys who wanted to start up a nightclub in Halifax. You may also remember that I said, 'The proposition was good and I actually believed that they would deliver it. Their market analysis was superbly researched . . .' I hope that by the time you have written about your markets and competition your readers are just as impressed.

Right, let me get a few fallacies out of the way very quickly. Many businesses justify their sales figures by one of the following arguments:

- 'We are only aiming to get 0.5 per cent of the UK market' – usually put forward by a new business in a new market with a new product or service. It just so happens that the total UK market for their product is estimated (by them) to be £1,000,000,000 and they are using this to justify their first-year projection of £5 million. What arrogant rubbish! We have seen this sort of approach fail – particularly with the recent dotcom companies that have spectacularly gone bump. There are two immediate flaws in their argument. First, they are not sure of the UK market size and so they are making assumptions about how they will gain market share in what may be a largely unknown marketplace. Second, if they were correct about the size of their market share and assuming a gradual build-up of sales (because that is how it usually works), Month 1 sales will be virtually nothing and Month 12 sales will be closer to £6 million or £7 million. This is close to 40 per cent more than they were initially forecasting and probably far beyond their ability to supply.

- 'Sales grew last year by 10 per cent so we will do the same again this year' – usually put forward by established businesses assuming that history can predict the future. Tell that to the guys at Perrier the year before they had their 'little spot of bother' with contamination in their product: the following year's sales were a fraction of the previous year's. As I have said before, no business has a God-given right to repeat any growth it has had before. There are too many variables that can upset this – your product, your customers, your competitors, the rest of the world. If you have had good growth the previous year that is excellent news. Analyse how you achieved it and see if you can repeat the process again this year – but be sure you know how it was achieved.

- 'We have increased our production capacity by 20 per cent so we should be able to sell, say, 15 per cent more' – why should increased capacity lead to increased sales? Only increased sales and marketing effort leads to more sales.

I hope I have convinced you that you really should spend a bit more time looking at customers, competitors and the world out there.

Market research – from the comfort of your own desk

If you have a new business or are attempting to get into a new market and are trying to make some forecast for your first year, then you have my utmost sympathy. Since you do not have any existing customers you can't ask them what they will buy next year. You can't look at how you have got new business before. You know nothing about your customers because you don't have any. In this situation you have no alternative but to make an educated estimate of what you might sell. Note that I said *educated* estimate and not wild guess or finger-in-the-air. However, recognise that this is a very impersonal way of forecasting and has a high potential for error.

So how do you do it? First, I am going to suggest that you think in terms of unit sales and not £sales at this stage. The reason for this is that £sales is the product of two variables: unit sales and price. I believe these should be dealt with separately. Right, let's follow the process using the example of a business trying to come up with a sales volume for computers in the UK.

1 What evidence can you find to support economic trends in general in the UK? At this stage you are trying to establish whether the economy is growing or contracting and to get any other pointers that may indicate whether people are likely to spend more money on computers. To start with, you could look at the *Annual Abstract of Statistics*, published by the Office for National Statistics. This gives indicators for the previous ten years, so trends can be seen. There may be other government-produced statistics that could help you. These will be shown in the *Guide to Official Statistics* published by the Stationery Office.

2 What evidence can you find to support demand for your product or service? At this stage you are looking for indicators that are more specific to computers (narrowing down from the general economy). Business monitors are produced by the government. These statistics are collected from UK firms. You may recall having received one of their monthly statistical returns in which they ask for figures such as turnover for that month, exports made, product description (using SIC codes, 'SIC'

standing for Standard Industrial Classification). There are a series of these monitors – one of which may include your product or service. The production monitors are produced regularly. The Service and Distribution Monitors cover the retail market and a whole range of others. The Annual Census of Production Monitors is very comprehensive and covers nearly every sector of industry, quantifying many aspects of economic activity within these. Key Note Ltd publish a range of 'Key Note' reports, which provide a comprehensive analysis of specific industries. This will include trends, average spends, market shares, how that particular industry works, recent developments. In addition an assessment of future growth within the industry is made.

3   What evidence is there to support any assessment of your marketplace? Having established the general economic trends and viewed any reports pertinent to computers, it is now time to focus on your market. *Acorn*, published by CACI Market Analysis, produces a classification of residential neighbourhoods. This analyses households by over fifty categories within postcodes. You could find out for every postcode within your geographic area key information relating to housing type, size of household, etc. This may help you to assess what may be happening at a general economic level within your market. If, however, your market is wider than this – the whole of the UK or even European – then you should also include *Consumer Europe* and *European Consumer Brands and their Owners*, published by Euromonitor. These provide data on thousands of products – market size, production, main brand information, and even some forecast data.

4   Finally, it is time to make an assessment of what your business may sell based on the evidence you have found so far. This means taking your assessment of the local marketplace for computers (gained from Steps 1 to 3 above) and looking at the competition to assess what they may be supplying. Your direct competitors and potential customers can be obtained from *Key British Enterprises*, published by Dun and Bradstreet. It includes information on some 50,000 UK companies, such as contact details, branch details, products sold (using SIC codes), sales turnover, number of employees, trade names, etc.

I should also mention *Kompass*, which indexes products/services by suppliers (Volume 1) and data on each of these (Volume 2). *The Retail Directory*, published by Newman Books, identifies all the UK department stores and privately owned shops together with contact details. It also contains some product-related data. (Other sources of information are included in the appendix.)

Market research – treading the street

If none of the published data gives you what you want, then there is no alternative but to find out the information you need directly – by asking people. This may be the case for a new product/service/market where no such information exists. There are several of ways of achieving this:

- Do it yourself. You may recall the example of the guys who wanted to start up a nightclub in Halifax, whose market research impressed me. They visited the local pubs and clubs (competitor analysis) to assess how busy they were and what they offered. They interviewed young people (using a questionnaire) and asked them where they came from, how frequently they came for a night out in Halifax, why they used the various clubs and pubs, what they liked and disliked and what they would want from a new club (customer survey). When they collated and analysed the questionnaires they found out that they had hit a veritable rich seam.

- Pay someone else to do it for you. If you don't feel confident enough to find out what you need to know, commission someone else to do it for you. If you are on a limited budget why not use local final-year marketing students. You may find that if you contact a local college and speak to a senior marketing lecturer they will recommend some students (usually their best) who can do the leg work for you. You can discuss with them what you want to achieve and let them get on with it. If you are fortunate enough to have a bigger budget then use a professional market research company. If you don't know of one then contact the Market Research Society and they will give you a list and can offer advice on how to conduct research.

- Share the costs with someone else. If you need a professional to help you but you are frightened off by the cost, which may be several thousand pounds, why not share the cost? Basically, several complementary or competing businesses pay for a survey to be carried out for them by one market-research company. You tell the researchers what questions you want answered and they add them to their questionnaire. These surveys are usually carried out face to face but may include telephone surveys if this is more practical or cost-effective. Because you are sharing the research the costs are much lower but you do have to wait until the parties to the research are on board.

These 'omnibus' surveys are offered by companies such as MORI and NOP. If you contact them directly they will be able to tell you of any forthcoming surveys so that you can piggyback on these if they are of interest to you. The cost of these surveys is typically £300–£600, dependent on the number of questions you want to ask, and are used for more general surveys.

Another approach is to use a 'specialist survey'. These are carried out less frequently than general surveys – typically quarterly. Your questions are charged on a per-question basis and a panel of captive respondents complete them. The panels are supposed to be representative to give you a valid response, and vary in size between a few hundred and a few thousand. These specialist surveys are, as their name implies, conducted by industry-specialist market-research agencies. The costs of these surveys vary according to the number of questions you want to ask and the size of the panel. You may be able to identify these by contacting the Market Research Society.

This will give you a good assessment of market trends for your product/service. Armed with this information you can then make some initial assessment of what volumes you might sell and selling prices (from competitor products). The next stage will be to work out your production costs and the resulting gross profit. While this is a valid approach to sales forecasting I must mention my earlier caveat: this approach can and does have a high degree of error. If I were using this approach I would be looking at very high sensitivities in my sensitivity analysis and would have a whole range of contingency plans if sales were only a small factor of those forecast.

Sales forecasts

Armed with knowledge about the marketplace in general, which either gives you confidence that things are improving or suggests that hard times are ahead, you should now try to construct a sales forecast.

Current and past customers

If your business already has customers (and most do) then they are a wealth of information for you.

Case study

I remember a client, who ran a civil engineering business near Luton, calling me to say how depressed he was about the next year ahead of him. It was at the time in the early 1990s that spending cuts by local councils were devastating the building and small-works marketplace. His gut feel was that the next year would see turnover down by 10 per cent to 20 per cent, which would mean laying people off and returning to loss making. I went down to see him and suggested that we review all his existing customers, some recent past customers and any possible clients. As we sat down we did the following with each customer:

1 We looked back over the last twelve months to see what pattern (if any) was apparent in their spending. Based on this analysis we made an initial estimate for the next year.
2 We phoned each customer to verify which contracts for work they had and where they wanted to use us. This was used to try to confirm our own estimate.
3 We looked at every council within our area and got their best estimate of their civil and small-works budget for the next twelve months and tried to assess how much of that our customers were likely to get. This was used to try to confirm that our customers would have work.
4 We then phoned every previous customer from the past twelve months to subject them to the same treatment as current customers.

At the end of this exercise we had a sales forecast for every customer – these were clearly identified customers. Overall, it appeared that sales over the next twelve months would be 20 per cent *higher* than the past year. When I spoke to this client later in the year he told me that he was in fact having a record year and that the sales forecast had given him real confidence to plan additional resources to handle this growth.

What do you want to sell?

Another approach that draws on past and current sales experience is to determine what you need to do to sell more to meet your new business objectives. For example, if last year's sales had been £150,000 and this year you were after a 20 per cent increase to £180,000, then the approach might be as follows:

1 Establish that it is possible to sell another £30,000. This can be done by looking at the market research mentioned earlier and reviewing your known competitors to see how they will behave. Hopefully, this will confirm that the additional sales are possible.

2 Establish what you have to do to sell another £30,000. This involves reviewing your sales and marketing activity to understand how you currently achieve sales. For example, if you rely on salespeople then you could look at their sales activity. If, say, you have one salesperson and they make thirty sales calls a week, out of which they get six appointments and achieve three sales of £960 each on average, you have some facts to work on.

Your 20 per cent increase can be achieved by improving any one (or all) of the five variables above (people, calls, appointments, sales, average sale value). A 4 per cent improvement in all of these would give the required 20 per cent increase in sales. If, however, extra people are required, then make sure your plan reflects this and acknowledge that new people will not be fully productive straight away.

Product life cycle

Another consideration must be where your products/services are in terms of their life cycle, because this will have an impact on your ability to sell them (and make profit from them). This is illustrated opposite.

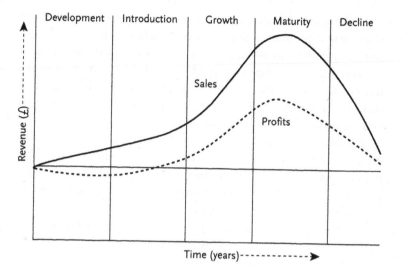

- Development: Lots of activity but none of it generating sales and all those boffins spending money hits the bottom line – net result is a loss-making period.

- Introduction: Amid panics – will the product be ready on time – it is launched with a massive (and costly) fanfare. Production has the headache of getting the product out and is generally making a mess of it. The first customers have bought (but are not happy) so sales revenues are trickling in.

- Growth: Lots of customers have now heard of the product (wow, the marketing is working) and the product is now really good (Well done, Production!). Sales are booming and production is slick – this is a recipe for really good profits (at last).

- Maturity: The product is now becoming a bit boring and the market is saturated – nearly everyone has got one now. Efforts are made to 'facelift' the product, which gives it a new lease life – but it can't last for ever. This extra cost hits profits and sales are starting to decline.

- Decline: By now competitors' products have overtaken it. The product is now old hat and only Rip Van Winkle (who has never seen anything like it before) is buying. Marketing is panicking and R&D have had all leave cancelled – they must come up with a new product fast. Profits have now nose-dived.

Looking at this analysis, can you spot where your products or services are in their life cycle and the effect it will have on your sales forecasts? If you are forecasting a 20 per cent growth in sales for each of the next five years, then your products probably need to be in the introduction stage – that way you may have three to four years before they start to decline. You may not even have two years if your products are hi-tech or in a similar fast-changing marketplace.

If, however, your products are already at the mature stage, dream on if you think you have five years of sales growth ahead of you! The point to remember is that no business can assume sales growth over a prolonged period of time without investment in new products or services. This will reduce your profitability.

As a final point on sales forecasts I want to look at two ways of forecasting sales growth depending on whether there is or is not any seasonality. If you can justify that your sales are going to grow, say, 20 per cent from £1,000,000 to £1,200,000, how should you show this in your sales forecast? There are two ways that have some merit.

No seasonality

If there is no seasonality to your annual sales then you should show a gradual build-up month by month to your extra £200,000 of sales. This will mean that by Month 12 you will be running at annualised sales of closer to £1,400,000.

Sales forecast showing growth from £1,000,000 p.a. to £1,200,000 p.a.

No seasonality

	Core sales		Growth	New sales	annualised
Month 1	£1,000,000/12 =	£83,333	£3,333	£86,666	£1,039,996
Month 2	£1,000,000/12 =	£83,333	£5,000	£88,333	£1,059,996
Month 3	£1,000,000/12 =	£83,333	£8,333	£91,666	£1,099,996
Month 4	£1,000,000/12 =	£83,333	£11,667	£95,000	£1,139,996
Month 5	£1,000,000/12 =	£83,333	£15,000	£98,333	£1,179,996
Month 6	£1,000,000/12 =	£83,333	£16,667	£100,000	£1,199,996
Month 7	£1,000,000/12 =	£83,333	£16,667	£100,000	£1,199,996
Month 8	£1,000,000/12 =	£83,333	£18,333	£101,666	£1,219,996
Month 9	£1,000,000/12 =	£83,333	£21,667	£105,000	£1,259,996
Month 10	£1,000,000/12 =	£83,333	£25,000	£108,333	£1,299,996
Month 11	£1,000,000/12 =	£83,333	£28,333	£111,666	£1,339,996
Month 12	£1,000,000/12 =	£83,333	£30,000	£113,333	£1,359,996
Total	£1,000,000		£200,000	£1,200,000	

Seasonality

But even this approach has some inaccuracies if there is a marked seasonality or volatility in monthly sales. If this is the case try to match the 20 per cent growth to each month as shown below:

Sales forecast showing growth from £1,000,000 p.a. to £1,200,000 p.a.

With seasonality

	Core sales	Growth	New sales
Month 1	£70,000	20%	£84,000
Month 2	£100,000	20%	£120,000
Month 3	£100,000	20%	£120,000
Month 4	£110,000	20%	£132,000
Month 5	£110,000	20%	£132,000
Month 6	£90,000	20%	£108,000
Month 7	£80,000	20%	£96,000
Month 8	£80,000	20%	£96,000
Month 9	£80,000	20%	£96,000
Month 10	£60,000	20%	£72,000
Month 11	£60,000	20%	£72,000
Month 12	£60,000	20%	£72,000
Total	£1,000,000		£1,200,000

In this case we can see the new sales forecast is still showing 20 per cent (£200,000), but it is allocated on a seasonal basis.

Current and proposed customers

Up to now we have talked about market research and selling, but you need customers to have a successful business. What do you know about your customers and potential customers? Unless you understand how they behave and what they need you have little chance of either getting them in the first place or keeping them thereafter. Here is a story that illustrates this.

Case study

Jeremy Yarwood set up his business, Embroidery Express, to sell personalised clothing primarily to local businesses. A business would need industrial clothing for its workforce. Jeremy's company would supply this embroidered with the company logo. For the customer there was a two-fold benefit: their workforce looked smarter, which enhanced the image of the business (professional look), and the staff liked the clothes, which they could use out of work without embarrassment (and without any taxable-benefit consequences). Jeremy had recently bought a larger multi-headed machine and really needed extra sales to fully justify its use. His local marketplace provided little scope for further growth, so he looked for fresh pastures.

He identified that Bristol, which was about fifty miles away, had sufficient industry to warrant his attention. Despite his mailshots and telesales efforts he had made no real impact. He was convinced that his offering was right – price, quality and service – but something was still *not* right. One day he was approached by a Bristolian girl (she had a lovely broad accent) who suggested that he needed to set up a local sales office – and that she should run it. What she said made sense, so he tried it.

Within three months the Bristol sales office was breaking even and has since gone on from strength to strength. Nothing had changed about the product but the difference was in the way he was meeting his customers' needs. They wanted to deal with a local firm – so a local voice, local telephone number and local address created that impression. The customers felt that they were getting a more personal service and that they could always 'drop in' to the office.

If Jeremy thinks 'customer focus' is important, so should you. Professor David Storey of the SME Centre at Warwick University conducted a survey of owner-managed businesses to find out what made them grow quickly (this study was entitled 'The Ten Percenters', because they were believed to be such a small group, and was commissioned by Deloitte & Touche). There was a belief that issues such as good management and training may be important – which they are. However, it soon became clear that the fastest-growing businesses had one thing in common: customer focus. They understood their customers very well and were totally committed to offering products and services that met their customers' needs.

Customer needs

You may think of your product or service as something tangible. Rolls-Royce may have argued that they made the best car in the world. But, if you had asked almost any adult male in the 1980s why he wanted an air-cooled Porsche 911, you would have almost smelled the testosterone in the air. This car, above almost any other, appealed to the emotions – despite being old-fashioned, an ergonomic nightmare, and having allegedly suspect handling. Customers are different and have different needs and you need to know this. This will help explain why you cannot sell a £100,000 car to some people no matter how much you discount it (even by 50 per cent). It's not that they don't want the car: it's rather that they have more pressing needs just now.

Maslow's Hierarchical Theory explains this. He was a psychologist who classified consumer needs as a five-stage process, known as the hierarchy of needs. These are shown in the diagram below.

Your products or services need to meet one or more of these needs. Your customers (like all human beings) progress upwards in this hierarchy. For example, only when they have satisfied their physiological needs, such as hunger, thirst and warmth, will they consider other needs. Bringing this back to a business level, it helps explain why certain types of business, such as supermarkets, are recession-proof, because they supply basic needs. It also explains why Porsche nearly went out of business during the 1980s recession, their product appealing to the highest of needs. Maybe this is something for you to consider.

Market segmentation

The world is too big for your average business to take on (unless of course you are a world player like Microsoft) so you need to break it down to a manageable size for you. This process of organising customers into groups with similar characteristics is known as market segmentation. In effect, you don't take on the whole world of customers but focus on segments that you can best satisfy. These segments are all quite unique in their needs. Typical market segmentation goes along the following lines:

Demographic segmentation

This groups customers together by personal attributes, such as age, sex, education, stage in the family life cycle, and socioeconomic groupings (A, B, C1, C2, D, E). These clearly have an effect on their needs and hence their ability to buy your product. Among these attributes the socioeconomic groupings are key:

Group	Social status	Occupation	Percentage of adults
A	Upper middle class	Higher managerial Administrative Professional	3
B	Middle class	Middle managerial Administrative Professional	10
C1	Lower middle class	Supervisory Clerical Junior managerial Administrative Professional	23
C2	Skilled working class	Skilled manual workers	33
C2	Working class	Semi- and unskilled manual workers	22
D	Subsistence level	Pensioners, widows Casual, lowest-paid workers	9

Can you clearly see which of these groups your product or service appeals to? If you can't you need to find out, otherwise you don't know whom you are selling to, which makes it difficult to get more customers. If you sell in the business-to-business market, then this demographic segmentation may not seem to be relevant. However, for this market, SIC (Standard Industrial Classification) categories, employee numbers, turnover size, etc. can be used as demographic descriptors.

Demographic segmentation helps to explain why luxury products, such as Rolls-Royce cars, have such a small (niche) market, as only some 3 per cent of the population are in a position to afford them, let alone buy one. On the other hand, products such as toothpaste are bought by everyone regardless of their socioeconomic class, which explains why they sell in such large volumes.

Geographic segmentation

As its name implies, this type of segmentation groups customers according to where they live and choose to buy. Quite clearly in many cases customers choose to buy locally. A good example is supermarket shopping. Most customers will use their nearest or most convenient (for car parking, for instance) supermarket to buy from. This also explains why retailers group together in retail parks to be near to large conurbations. However, there is a correlation among the level of spend, availability of the product and desirability of the product that can defeat geographic constraints. A good example would be dining out – especially in the evening. Fashionable restaurants can be located in areas such as the Cotswolds (in the middle of nowhere) and attract regular customers from as far away as Stratford upon Avon, Oxford and Cheltenham.

How will geography influence your customers? Will they travel to buy? Your first task is to recognise that this may affect sales of your product or service, and then you need to work out how you counter-act this problem. A classic example must be how retailers have used the Internet and mail order to extend the geographic areas into which they can sell.

Benefit segmentation

As its name implies, this recognises that not all customers get the same benefit from the same product or service. A good example is again provided by toothpaste. Some buy it because it makes their teeth sparkle (cosmetic benefit) and enhances their appeal to other people. On the other hand, millions of householders buy it for their family or household group to make sure their teeth are free from cavities (medical benefit). Some products aim to extend their sales by showing a standard benefit and a double benefit – like toothpaste.

There are two other benefit types that you should be aware of:

- Company benefit: Where the customer buys a product that satisfies an initial need but also buys a relationship with their supplier. Factors such as delivery, after-sales service, public perception and reputation all contribute to this. This is often the case with prestige sports cars, where advertising, motor racing, branded personal products (clothes, cosmetics, etc.) keep the buyer involved.

- Differential benefit: You must be able to demonstrate that your product or service is different from others, otherwise potential customers will not switch to yours. Customers will show remarkable brand loyalty, but, if you can demonstrate to them that your product or service is cheaper, better and quicker, they have a reason to buy from you.

All this talk of segmentation can be quite confusing. However, we can pull it all together to put it into perspective. There are three aspects to explaining why customers buy: what is bought (choice), why it is bought and who buys it. The table below shows how segmentation impacts on these:

Factors determining what is bought	Volume, price, distribution, physical characteristics, geography
Factors determining why it is bought	Benefits, attitudes, perceptions, preferences
Factors determining who buys	Brand loyalty, socioeconomic, demographic, lifestyles

Matching your product to your customers

Now that you know where your customers are, how do you ensure that your products or services are what they want or need? Marketing people often talk about features and benefits, which are important to the selling/buying process but are frequently confused by people.

Quite simply, features are what a product or service has or is, while benefits are what it does for your customer. When you are selling you must recognise which of these two is going to make your customer part with their money and offer the proof for the benefit being offered. The example below illustrates this:

Features	Our new car has a new direct injection diesel engine with a continuously variable automatic transmission.
Benefits	Our car offers better fuel economy than any other in its class, which means it is cheaper to run. Our new transmission means it is easier to drive and better performance because the engine has an infinite range of gears.
Proof	Department of Transport tests confirm fuel consumption. *What Car* and *Autocar* road tests have confirmed performance.

So this spells out the features and benefits that will help your customers to buy, but will they all arrive at the same time? Well, no, because another part of their uniqueness is *when* they buy. You will find that, despite extensive advertising that everyone has seen, some people buy right from the start while others hang back. This is even more apparent with new products or services. In fact, volume sales cannot be achieved until the innovators or early adopters (the early buyers) have signified acceptance of the product so that the rest of the buying population can safely follow.

A classic example of this was Sir Clive Sinclair's C5 single-seater car. This was cheap and innovative. Unfortunately, it did not get the 'sign of approval' from the early buyers and was not a commercial success. How will this affect your new products or services? Until you get past the early takers you will not get into the high-volume sales.

Competitor analysis

By now you should have a pretty good idea of who your customers will be and their specific needs. There are, however, some people standing between you and this pot of gold – they are your competitors. They have the same objectives as you and if you are to succeed you have to defeat them. You ignore them at your peril. Once again, intelligence is the key. What do you know about them? When you can size up your competitors then you can decide on the right action to take.

Case study

Some years ago I was talking to a kitchen unit manufacturer about competitor analysis. He had been going through a particularly difficult period, with competitors apparently springing up overnight and taking away market share. Just recently a rather more serious competitor had emerged who was threatening his very existence. Deciding that he could not ignore this threat, he determined to find out more about them. His research was as follows.

First of all he asked around about them – customers, competitors, suppliers, his drivers, etc. The word on the street was that this new competitor was an established business but that there had been a recent management buy-out. Obviously, with additional funding they were flexing their muscles and trying to buy market share with what my friend called 'silly prices' and other deals. Wondering how big this new war chest was he decided to do a bit more rooting around. Who had invested in his competitor and how much had they put in?

He went to the business library at Warwick University (which is excellent) and asked the librarian how he could find out more about his competitors. What he discovered was quite amazing. There were financial databases, newspaper extracts, etc., all available on computer. He searched through all the national papers to find any articles about this new competitor. Sure enough, there was a big article in the financial press about the investment that a venture capital house had made. Reading a bit further, he noticed that most of the money had in fact been provided as loans – which as you remember have interest charges. In fact, to my friend's mind, the loan repayments looked massive.

The next stage was to dig out their accounts – again using the computer. Sure enough, over the last few years this business had underperformed and had run up large debts. A quick analysis convinced my friend that a lot of this new money had gone into paying off old creditors and buying out the previous owners. The reality was that only about £100,000 was available to fund an aggressive sales effort – which was what they were now engaged in.

My friend now felt he had the measure of his new competitor

because of this new intelligence. He decided that some sort of delaying tactics were required to wear out his competitor financially. The plan was to avoid bidding against him at silly non-profitable prices. This meant that if my friend were successful in his tenders he would make some profit (but not much) and that if he lost them to this new competitor he was confident that they were making no profit (because of their increased interest costs).

The battle was protracted, but after about twelve months this competitor suddenly disappeared and the local market settled down again. He saw in the newspaper that, owing to unsustainable profits, his competitor had decided to pull out of the marketplace and concentrate its efforts elsewhere.

The purpose of your competitor analysis is to size up your competitors. How many of them are there out there? How big are they? How profitable are they? What are their products like? The first stage is to identify who your competitors are. If you know who they are, all well and good – but it is quite possible that you *don't* know who they are. A good starting point is a business directory, such as *Kelly's*, *Kompass* and *Key British Enterprises* (we mentioned the last two earlier). These are available in most libraries and will tell you who's out there, what products or service they have, broadly how much they sell and how many employees they have. Not a bad start – now you know who the enemy are.

The next stage is to evaluate these competitors. If your initial research has identified a handful of potential competitors then you can fully research them all. If, however, it turns up, say, more than a dozen competitors, you may have to narrow it down a little. Choose only those that appear to be direct competitors for the full analysis – the peripheral competitors you look at later. The next stage must be to perform some financial analysis to see how strong these competitors appear to be. This can be done in one of two ways. The first we have already referred to – using a financial database.

I want to recommend two particular financial databases that will be available at either your nearest business school library or possibly via your business link/chamber of commerce. These are OneSource and FAME. They take annual accounts that have been filed at Companies House for both small and large limited companies and, as well as the 'raw' accounts, subject them to ratio analysis to enable you to make an assessment of the financial strength. If you can't interpret financial information get a friend to help you. The beauty of these two financial databases is they are so flexible. I have used them to find competitors as well as analyse them. They enable you to search for companies by any 'handle' or combination of these you want. For example you could search for all travel agents (using the SIC code), within a postcode area, with a turnover within the band £1–5 million per annum, that are making better than 10 per cent net profit in the last three years.

Periodically, reports are done on various industries. ICC Information Ltd provide these. The reports are quite expensive (around £250), but they are comprehensive. All the hard work is done for you – some twenty-plus performance ratios are calculated. All the businesses are rated – the best and the worst. You may even see your business included in here – which will give you a chance to see how well you compare with your competitors.

Whatever approach you take, and I have suggested just a few, your aim is to be wise to the competition. If you know who they are and how strong they are you are better placed to compete against them. Of course, the analysis I have suggested is mostly financial, although you should have found out something about their products and services as well. However, there are other things you may want to find out such as:

- Quality of their products or services
- Warranties and service
- Credit terms
- Reputation

So how do you find out about these? Well, this is something that you can do or enlist a friend or relative to help you. Phone them up directly and ask for a brochure and a reference site – pretend you are interested in buying from them. Ask around your customers and suppliers. Between this lot you should be able to find out everything you need to know.

Chapter summary

In this chapter we have learned how:

- You can undertake your own market research using information that is freely available in ordinary libraries and specialist libraries – show the key results (summary) of this in your business plan and the detailed research in the appendices.

- To get outside help to do your market research for you if you don't have the time or skills to do it yourself.

- To prepare a sales forecast taking account of existing customer profiles, seasonality and life cycle of your product or service – include a summary of your sales forecast in your business plan and the detailed forecasts in the appendices.

- To understand better what your customers' needs are using the hierarchy of needs.

- To understand the different backgrounds of your customers, which will influence what they buy – include in your business plan where your customers will come from.

- To identify and analyse your competitors so that you can defeat them – include in your business plan how you will defeat your competitors.

CHAPTER EIGHT

What's so special about your business?

Chapter outline

Now you have identified your customers and have a good idea what they want, you need to take them away from your competitors' clutches. Somehow you need to tell them about your product or service and convince them that yours is better, quicker, cheaper, etc. so that they want to buy from you rather than your competitors. You will also need to be honest with yourself and assess how well your business performs and what threats and opportunities lie ahead of it (SWOT: strengths, weaknesses, opportunities, threats). At the same time you need to be aware of what is going on outside your business (we call this environmental scanning). This chapter looks at competitive business strategy (making your business different from your competitors'), SWOT, PEST (this acronym is explained later) and the marketing mix. By the end of this chapter you will have identified what makes your business different and how you can get the marketing mix just right to maximise your sales.

Which parts of the business plan are covered in this chapter?

Section heading	What's covered in this section	Full business plan (external – raising money)	Full business plan (internal – performance enhancement)	Full business plan (internal – board approval)	Summary plan (external – lease, suppliers, etc.)
Competitive business strategy	PEST – environmental scanning	Yes	Yes	Yes – but see comment below	No
	SWOT analysis	Yes	Yes	Yes – but see comment below	No

Section heading	What's covered in this section	Full business plan (external – raising money)	Full business plan (internal – performance enhancement)	Full business plan (internal – board approval)	Summary plan (external – lease, suppliers, etc.)
	Contingency planning	Yes	Yes	No	No
	Marketing strategy	Yes	Yes	No	No
	Price, promotion and place	Yes	Yes	No	No
	Channels of distribution	Yes	Yes	No	No
Comments	This section should convince the reader that you will be successful because you know what is going on.	Must be very comprehensive and not leave unanswered questions.	Must be very comprehensive and not leave unanswered questions.	They already know your business, so limit the detail.	Tell them nothing – this is none of their concern, unless they ask.

Competitive business strategy

I know that the word 'strategy' is a much used, abused and misunderstood word but it is key to your business success. At this stage I am going to suggest that you need something that will start to pull together all the things that must be running round in your head. Your initial research has revealed quite a lot about markets, customers, competitors and possible sales forecasts. What you need now is a bit more focus that convinces both you and the reader of your business plan that there is something special about your business and that you know exactly how you are going to satisfy your target customers with your product or service.

We call this having a competitive business strategy and quite simply it determines what makes your business different from the others and why it will succeed. How are you going to make sure that your customers know about you and want to buy from you?

To keep this all in focus I want you to think about the model overleaf, which shows the linkage between business objectives, marketing and financial projections. The diagram shows that while marketing strategy is at the heart of making your business different, it must all fit within your mission and business objectives.

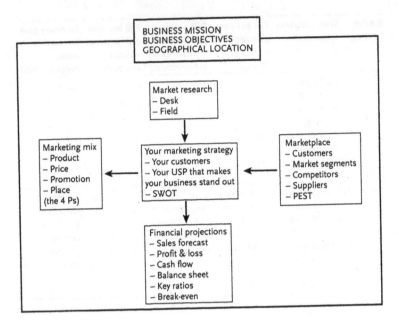

All of your business activities are determined by and must come within your business mission, objectives and geographical area of activity. Within this you gather market research to form a view on your marketplace. This enables you to form your marketing strategy. The delivery of this marketing strategy is via your marketing mix and the financial projections are the anticipated results of your marketing strategy. All very simple, really – but how do you make it all happen?

Environmental scanning – PEST

Customers and competitors are all very close to home, but what else may have an impact on your business life? You need to be scanning the horizon to see what other curved balls are about to strike you down. You cannot ignore what is going on in the rest of the UK, Europe and the world – even if your business is confined to, say, the Midlands. Changes in any of the following may have an impact on your business:

Customers: Changing fashions and fads, shifts in spending power (changes in socioeconomic groupings), changing priorities – all affect demand.

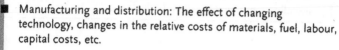

- Workforce: Changing aspirations, skills, remuneration expectations (as a result of increased living costs), and education – all affect human resources.

- Manufacturing and distribution: The effect of changing technology, changes in the relative costs of materials, fuel, labour, capital costs, etc.

- Communications (internal and external): Technology will again affect this.

With a focus firmly fixed on these areas what should we scan the environment for? What changes should we be on the lookout for? The areas are covered by the acronym PEST, which is made up of these headings:

Political pressures

- UK government – what is their attitude to business? Are they supportive of a competitive free-market economy or are they interfering and restrictive (introducing lots of red tape, for instance)?

- What pressures are there on health and safety, environment protection and consumer protection leading to possible new laws that may affect you?

- Employment – will there be new legislation that may shift the balance towards either the employer or employee?

- Race relations – is this stable or will new legislation be needed to enforce better balance?

- Europe – how is the balance shaping up between the UK and Europe? Are we about to see a shift in power leading to new European legislation affecting you?

Economic pressures

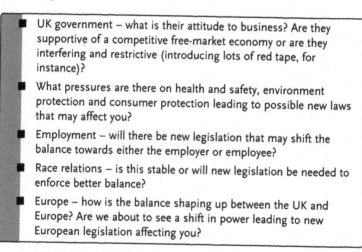

- Boom or recession – what do the economic indicators suggest is ahead for the UK as a whole and your industry in particular? What about interest rates, inflation, growth?

- The pound v. euro v. US dollar – how are exchange rates moving? Do these favour you as an exporter or importer?

- Employment – is this a period of full employment (may be bad for you as an employer) or high unemployment (which may be better for you as an employer)? Can you get the skills you need?

> ■ Spending power – do your target groups still have the same spending power? Has there been a shift from old to young, big business to small business, etc.? Are government departments spending – or tightening their budgets?

Social pressures

> ■ Quality of life – are people experiencing improvements in life at home and work and in society in general? Will this affect your business?
>
> ■ Employment – are workers expecting to have more involvement in decisions, management, control of their work environment? How might this affect you?
>
> ■ Changing social structure – what effect does the changing structure of households have on you, e.g. the increase in one-parent families, two-income households, etc.
>
> ■ Green lobby – are consumers becoming more socially aware? Do they demand greener, cleaner goods and services? Will this affect you?

Technological pressures

> ■ Communications – how will new technology change the way customers, suppliers and staff interact? Is there a major change about to hit your industry?
>
> ■ Manufacturing/service delivery – is your product or service under threat and about to become obsolete as new technology creates new more innovative and cheaper products and services?
>
> ■ Banking – how will changes like electronic banking affect the way your business trades? If you don't have the latest ways of paying, will it affect your business?

So you have gathered this information. What do you want to do with it? Well, certainly don't ignore the information if it points to something significant. You need to assess the likely impact that your PEST analysis has uncovered and your response to this threat. Perhaps the example below will show you how you should approach this.

Beechwood Enterprises Limited, you may recall, was a new-start metal finisher. This business is a nasty business – I know because I was involved in it for four years. The key ingredients are thoroughly nasty chemicals, which are first used to clean the base metal and then to help the coating process. In the old days these were dumped into a waste tank and drip-fed into the waste-water system – a cheap and cheerless solution.

As a result of their PEST analysis it became very apparent that impending legislation was going to change all this within eighteen months (this was the threat). The new legislation effectively closed down the dumping option. It meant that metal finishers (and all other businesses) were to be responsible for their waste. All water authorities were tasked with monitoring the waste that flowed into their rivers and other watercourses. This meant that every business was under constant scrutiny – pollute and you get fined and closed down (this was the impact). This was not an option for this company.

As part of their business planning process Beechwood Enterprises incorporated a recycling and treatment facility for their process (this was the response). It cost £50,000 (all budgeted for) and, while not state of the art, it was effective. It did, however, put up their cost base but it did have one pleasant side effect: it put out of business the back-street metal finishers. In fact, this whole business segment moved more upmarket and within twelve months pricing levels had shifted to recover these costs.

Assessing the options – SWOT

An important part of creating your marketing strategy must be first to establish what you are good at so that your marketing strategy plays to this. Now of course no business is universally strong in all areas of its operation – don't worry, because if you recognise some weaknesses you can do something about them. However, if some of your weaknesses are pretty fundamental then it is best to recognise them now and look for a new marketing strategy. At the same time you should examine the wider world around you to see what threats and opportunities lie out there. This process is known as SWOT analysis because it looks at Strengths, Weaknesses, Opportunities and Threats. Let's illustrate this with an example that came from our old friends Beechwood Enterprises:

SWOT analysis

		Strengths	Weaknesses
1	Customers	They love us and they come back for more	We don't have enough for future growth
2	Product or service	It's well regarded and sells well	It's at its maturity stage and needs replacing
3	Place	We are very close to our customers with good access and parking	Our offices are a bit of an eyesore to visitors
4	Promotion	We get referrals by word of mouth	We don't do very much to promote the business
5	Price	Our price is competitive but at times we are not the cheapest	We don't monitor competitor prices
6	Finance	We make 15 per cent net profit and have £30,000 cash reserves	If we were to grow at 20 per cent next year we might be tight on cash
7	Operations	Our production facilities and work done is second to none	We are only working at 50 per cent capacity

Identifying strengths and weaknesses is all about looking *inwards* to see what you are good at (so you can do more of this) and what you are bad at (so you can avoid doing this or find some way of doing it better). Be honest when you carry out this exercise and do get more than one person to carry it out – I suggest your management team 'brainstorm' on this.

Looking *outwards*, our friends at Beechwood Enterprises have identified the following opportunities and threats:

		Opportunities	Threats
8	Economic	The economy is projected to grow at 5 per cent per annum over the next 5 years	This level of growth would not support our 20 per cent per annum growth ambitions
9	Political	The government is supportive of small business	The environmental lobby makes our life difficult and threatens more legislation
10	Competitors	They seem to be smaller and less professional than us	A big player from Birmingham may see our marketplace as attractive

Armed with this additional knowledge the managers of Beechwood Enterprises can start to plan marketing actions that draw on the business strengths, minimise the weaknesses, counter the external threats and seize on the opportunities. They can now put together an action plan. Below we see an extract from Beechwood Enterprises' action plan:

SWOT reference	Action	Complete by/who responsible
SWOT 1: Grow our customer base by 20 per cent next year	(1) Carry out market research to identify new customers within 30-mile radius	May 2001 PJB
	(2) Mailshot businesses identified by (1)	Jun 2001 PJB
	(3) Follow up mailshot with phone call	June/July 2001 REB
	(4) Make initial calls	Aug 2001 SLB

Of course, you must evaluate the costs and benefits of the actions necessary to complete this. The costs are not just the immediately obvious, such as stationery and phone calls, but should include the less obvious. These could include the human resources – can we spare PJB, REB and SLB for these actions? Also, have you included the capital cost of the new software and new laser printer needed to do the mailshots?

Of course, if there are a whole range of actions that need to be taken to achieve success you will need to focus on those that are most critical to your business's success. Quite frequently a business will compare their own product or service against their main competitor's using what they believe to be the critical success factors (CSF). Overleaf we can see how Beechwood Enterprises has done this.

Of course, unless you can get some outside verification of these assessments then they are going to be a bit subjective. It may help if you get all of your staff to contribute so you get a wider view. It may also be really worthwhile to ask your customers what they think of you as against your competitors. It is amazing what home truths may crawl out of the woodwork. This CSF showed that Competitor C was better than Beechwood Enterprises on the overall service rating – that came as a bit of a shock!

Competitors / Critical Success Factors	Weighting factor %	Your Business	Competitor A	Competitor B	Competitor C
		All scores on a scale of 0 = very poor to 10 = excellent			
Price of service	50%	7	5	5	8
Quality of service	30%	9	7	6	8
Convenience	20%	6	6	6	6
Total Weighted Score	100%	7.4	5.8	5.5	7.6

We have used Beechwood Enterprises as an example but you will need to look long and hard at your business using SWOT. You should be able to identify your strengths and weaknesses since these should be reasonably apparent to you and your team. The difficult areas are the opportunities and threats, which involve looking outwards. In particular I would invite you to be very thorough when looking for threats because to counter these you will need contingency plans.

Contingency planning

There is a chance that things may not go according to plan. In fact things seldom do – be honest, you know that anyway. Now you may think you have got this covered by the sensitivity analysis that we covered at the tail end of Chapter Five. But to be honest this really covers only the minor mishaps, e.g. what if some of our customers don't buy as much as we are forecasting? What if there were a recession – how would you fare? What if a competitor becomes really aggressive and decides to cut margins? These are the nasties that could come out of your SWOT analysis.

...y

...id of mine was facing exactly this last situation. Up until ...his business had been growing and was moving into small but ...ing profits. Turnover was now approaching £1 million. He had invested in state-of-the-art equipment that was better than most of the big players he competed with. On the face of it things looked reasonably rosy – especially if he could continue growing sales at similar margins. At the same time the UK was experiencing good growth – the period in question was early 2000. Then suddenly out of the blue I got a phone call from Jeremy – who did not sound his usual chipper self. Apparently his whole world was collapsing. Bit by bit I teased it out of him. He had lost a couple of big contracts and suddenly he had far too much capacity. He was chasing work and finding that to get it he had to slash margins. His competitors, it seemed, had polarised round the very large (£20 million and upwards) and the very small (one person and a machine operating out of a garage). Jeremy's original business plan was suddenly looking impossible. He was phoning me because he wanted to bounce some ideas off me – he needed a cunning plan, certainly one that was very different from his current business plan.

We talked for about two hours on the phone and came up with a range of options, which were:

1   Sell the business to any competitor that would buy it – or parts of it. Basically this was a get-out-at-almost-any-cost approach. He could sell his customers to anyone who wanted to buy turnover and his equipment to someone who needed better equipment. His premises he could sell privately. This was the least attractive option – but if he really was as cheesed off with his business as he said he was, it did at least give him a relatively quick get-out. There were other business ideas open to him – none, unfortunately, that he could merge this business with to reduce costs (another one of my ideas).

2   A joint venture with either a supplier who wanted to move further up the supply chain, or a competitor with whom he could offer complementary products (with minimal overlap). This way he retained some independence and had a

way of growing the business. There would be the possibility of selling his business in a couple of years' time to the joint venture partner.

3   Accelerate his own growth plan to get to £2 million turnover in double-quick time. This would require additional investment in human resources and working capital. A problem with this option was that it had no certainty – he could be in the same situation in 18 months' time, having increased his overheads. It was, however, an option – but for Jeremy it was not a favoured option.

The current situation is that Jeremy is investigating some of these options. You might, of course, ask why a big business would be interested in a small business that they could eventually pick off. Fair question – and one I had asked Jeremy. He had spotted that they had previously bought businesses like his (so they might be interested) and they were missing out on some markets that he could help them to get to.

Now I have not used Jeremy as a sorry story – he will end up smelling of muck eventually. I do, however, feel that you should take note and say to yourself, 'What would happen if my business plan got shot to hell through circumstances beyond my immediate control?'

Maybe you should look at your proposed business plan and ask yourself the following questions:

How do I make my business recession-proof?

One of the worst things that could happen is that you prepare a business plan that depends on growth for success. The typical feature of this type of plan is that break-even point rises as overhead costs (investment in growth) increase. But what if the bottom fell out of the market? How would you cope if your sales fell by 20 per cent in a matter of months and margins were reduced by 20 per cent? This would decimate your profit and cash-flow forecasts.

Can you quickly make yours a smaller but profitable business – put growth on the back burner for a couple of years? What actions do you need to take to secure your business? I don't know the specific plan for your business but it could include overhead reduction; selling surplus assets; calling in all favours owed; looking for niches (that are holding up well) rather than mass markets (that are suffering).

What if my product or service gets wiped out suddenly?

This must be an even bigger body blow than a recession – at least a recession hits everybody, this one is personal to you and your business. If the wipe-out comes as a result of a fashion or technology change or legislation then I have to say, 'Sorry, but why did your SWOT analysis not reveal this?' You should have been forewarned. Hopefully your research and development has a new product or service nearly ready in the wings – it's just a matter of speeding things up a bit to get it into the marketplace. If you are not developing new products or services all the time then I have to say you are living dangerously – this is your wake-up call to get back into the real world. A colleague of mine said something that really stuck in my mind. The challenge of every business is to profit from change. Customers will always want a product or service to be faster, cheaper, better, etc. Your challenge as a business is to be able to provide them with this – and still make a profit.

This means that the reality is that your product or service will become redundant – it's just a matter of when this will happen. If you have this to the forefront of your mind and plan to replace all your products and services you will not go far wrong.

What if my market disappears overnight?

It does not happen very often, fortunately, but sometimes a whole marketplace for a product or service disappears. There is nothing wrong with the product or service – it's still as good as ever. The problem is that the niche has disappeared or the need for the product has gone. I guess this is a warning for all businesses that are targeting niches – what happens when it has gone? The answer must be to ensure that you are always scanning the market for new niches and products to fill them.

This was the issue that faced many small backstreet garages in the late 1980s. Cars were starting to be more reliable and needed fewer repairs. Also, at the same time, all the mass manufacturers of cars were moving to computerised diagnostics – which meant that without the right equipment you could not service these cars. To further compound matters the franchised dealers were trying harder to get back those customers by offering cheaper rates for older cars.

To stay in business these backstreet garages had to invest a lot of money in technology – for a limited return. For many small garages this was the final straw and many just closed down. They were already marginal businesses but now it was impossible to make money. Fortunately, mass markets tend not to disappear suddenly, but they do change and disappear over a few years. Watch the trends and be ready.

What happens if I can't get the people I need?

I have already flagged up the fact that people are a key part of any business – you are generally scuppered without them. If your growth plan says you need ten more salespeople over the next three years but so far you have not been able to recruit a single one, what do you do? I guess you will have tried all the recruitment tricks, such as upping the package, golden handcuffs, etc. Let's assume the calibre of sales-person that you want is in short supply or does not exist – what do you do? This is exactly the problem that Johnsons Coaches had.

Case study

Pete and John Johnson ran Johnsons Coaches, a fast-growing travel business. As part of their growth plan they needed more coach drivers. When they recruited they were generally dismayed at the low standard of applicants. This meant that they frequently had to accept people who were not of the standard they wanted – quality was important to them. The problem was that good drivers don't change jobs too often and they did not want to get into a turf war with other operators by poaching their good drivers.

Pete and John applied a bit of lateral thinking to the problem and decided to start up their own in-house drivers' school. They took on something like three trainees in the first year and ended up with two good drivers, who stayed. They made sure that the trainee drivers signed up to a contract that kept them for a period after the training – otherwise they had to pay back the training costs. Over the years they have 'grown' their own drivers. What it has meant is that they are largely protected from recruitment prob-lems because they can take almost anyone and convert them into useful members of the team.

Perhaps you can do what Pete and John did. When they did their SWOT analysis a shortage of drivers came up as a major threat. They thought around the problem – there is always a solution. Now I don't know all the questions you should be asking yourself – but I suspect you do. If you don't, then you need to be among people who know what is going on in your industry. Talk to your customers, suppliers, etc. to find out what is going on. Be prepared for change.

Marketing strategy

Somewhere out of all this analysis you need to establish some sort of marketing strategy for your business. There are basically only three recognised approaches:

- Cost leadership: A common approach taken by large multinational companies, with worldwide production and markets. Requires large-scale capital investment. Often low-margin products but that's because these companies operate very efficiently. They create barriers to entry by low pricing. The classic example of this is motor vehicle manufacture, with VW Audi Group being a particularly good example. They have brand names such as VW, Audi, Seat and Skoda within the 'family', which are assembled throughout the world using common platforms (chassis) and engines – only the bodies are different.

- Differentiation: This approach relies on design, quality and image, and aims to establish strong brand loyalty. Quite often this approach creates unique products which have high margins. A good example of this must be the branded bottled waters – which have negligible cost but cost as much as the more-expensive-to-produce flavoured fizzy drinks such as Coca-Cola.

- Niche: This is where a business targets just one particular market. They do it efficiently with low costs and high margins. They establish a reputation and hope to maintain barriers to entry because of the small size of the market (or niche) that they are serving. Good examples of this are the businesses that have focused just on the replacement-windscreen market. With most motorists suffering a broken screen only once every twenty years or so (although I seem to have one every couple of years) this is not big enough to entice the screen manufacturers to enter it. The cost of setting up the depots and hundreds of kitted-out vans to support this service make it prohibitive to enter. Remember that if you go for the niche option it must be big enough and profitable enough to sustain your business and enable growth.

Having decided on one of these three basic marketing strategies you will need to create a unique selling proposition (USP) that makes you and your product stand out from your competitors. If yours is a 'me too' product then there is no good reason why anyone should buy from you. Essentially you have these options:

- **Quicker:** Customers will buy from you because you do it more quickly, e.g. Kwik-Fit, which trades on the boast that you 'can't get quicker than a Kwik-Fit fitter'.
- **Better:** Customers buy from you because they perceive you to be better, e.g. Pickfords trade on their careful-mover image.
- **Nicer:** Customers buy from you because they like dealing with you, e.g. the corner shop, where the owner serves personally and knows his customers' every need.
- **Cheaper:** Customers buy from you because you are dirt-cheap, e.g. the majority of small-scale double-glazing/replacement window companies.

The four Ps – product, price, promotion, place

Price

This is the $64,000 question: how much should you charge for your product or service? This is a problem that I have every time I get a chance to pitch for some new work for a client who has been referred to me. I am a consultant so I am selling my time. Of course, my time has a different cost according to a simple matrix:

- What do I think the value will be to my client? If I perceive that the solution that I will provide has high value to him then it will have a higher charge-out rate (and vice versa).
- How keen am I to do the work? Do I need or want the work (prestige client)? This will influence my pricing.
- What can I get away with? I look them in the eyes and try to assess how much they will go up to (a bit like poker). I say a price – and then curse when they agree quickly because I then know that I could have charged more.

Even in my simple situation it is difficult to arrive at the right price and avoid putting off the client while at the same time maximising my profits.

What then are the issues that you need to take into account when you determine the pricing for your product or service? There are two basic approaches:

1 **The accountant's approach:** First of all you work out the full cost of the product, including an allocation of overheads. You then decide on a standard mark-up, say 25 per cent, which you add on to the full costs and – hey presto! – you have a selling price. The problem is that if you sell at that price you will not get any customers because it is probably too high.

2 **The marketeer's approach:** You do market research to see what competitors are selling similar products or services at. You compare features and benefits and decide on a price either to undercut these products or to place yours above them. The problem is that if you sell at this price you may not make any profit.

There is a certain logic that suggests to me that a combination of the two may be the best approach. You start with the marketeer's approach to achieve the market share objective and follow up with the accountant's approach to ensure that reasonable profit can be made. Of course, you will know by now that you really should be looking at break-even as well – which places the focus on direct costs, fixed costs and changing revenues.

Other factors that you should take into account are:

■ Business objectives: It may be that previous products or services have been unprofitable and this time a higher profit has to be made to ensure the success of the business. Of course, if this leads to a higher price then some marketing objectives may have to be sacrificed – such as market share.

■ Product life cycle: As you may recall products go through five distinct cycles (development, introduction, growth, maturity, decline – see Chapter Eight). At each of these stages different pricing may apply according to the business need. For example, a product in its maturity stage would be ripe for profit maximisation – the focus would not be on improving market share. A similar approach may also be taken when a product is in a high-growth stage, the argument being that, since demand is so strong, higher pricing will not significantly dampen this.

■ Product positioning: The price should be compatible with the image of the product. For example, if the product were positioned as a high-quality, exclusive item it would be counterproductive to price it too low. This image can be created by actual physical properties or clever marketing.

■ Competition: Most products have competitors – although many companies try to make comparisons difficult by varying the

> combination of price, features and benefits. Your product will find it difficult to succeed if it appears to be the same as an identical product costing, say, 20 per cent less. Also, by pricing high you make it possible for new products to enter the marketplace – further compounding the problems.
>
> ■ Channels of distribution: If your product reaches the customer through a series of intermediaries – producer, wholesaler, retailer – then each of these needs a profit margin to pay for its services. Of course, the end price to your customer must be the same regardless of how it is distributed. Hence the producer must reduce his selling price to the first intermediary to enable sufficient margin to be available to pay for the rest of the distribution channel.

A question that always comes up in any discussion on pricing is discounting – should you ever discount your prices? I have very strong views on discounting. If you are an SME (small or medium-sized enterprise) then I am dead against discounting prices. Your customers generally buy from you on the basis of service, flexibility and quality. If you discount your selling price you are giving away net profit at an alarming rate. You need only to look at the Pricing Ready Reckoner (below) to see the effect of discounting prices.

Price Reduction Ready Reckoner – Sales needed to maintain Gross Margin

% Price Reduction	Existing Gross Margins (%)								
	5	10	15	20	25	30	35	40	50
2	67	25	15	11	9	7	6	5	4
3	150	43	25	18	14	11	9	8	6
4	400	67	36	25	19	15	13	11	9
5		100	50	33	25	20	17	14	11
7.5		300	100	60	43	33	27	23	18
10			200	100	67	50	40	33	25
15				300	150	100	75	60	43

% Volume of Extra Sales required 'to stand still'

Price Increase Ready Reckoner

% Price Increase	Existing Gross Margins (%)								
	5	10	15	20	25	30	35	40	50
2	29	17	12	9	7	6	5	5	4
3	37	23	17	13	11	9	8	7	6
4	44	29	21	17	14	12	10	9	7
5	50	33	25	20	17	14	12	11	9
7.5	60	43	33	27	23	20	18	16	13
10	67	50	40	33	29	25	22	20	17
15	75	60	50	43	37	33	30	27	23

% Volume Decrease in Sales required 'to stand still'

Using the ready reckoner as a guide you can see (top half) the effect of price discounting. Imagine, for example, that your product or service has a gross margin of 15 per cent – what would be the effect of discounting your sales price by just 10 per cent. Yes – you can believe your eyes. You would have to do another 200 per cent more business just to make the same overall profit as before. Is this the most solid argument against discounting? What it shows is that people seldom fully recognise the effect on profit of discounting selling prices.

Another option might be to consider putting up prices. Again looking at the ready reckoner (bottom half) we can see the effect of increasing prices. Imagine again that your product or service has a gross margin of 15 per cent – what would be the effect of increasing your sales price by just 10 per cent. If you lost no more than 40 per cent of your sales revenues you would be better off! In fact if your sales revenue fell by, say, just less than 40 per cent, you would be much better off because your business would make stock and debtor funding savings.

Promotion

Unless you want your product or service to be one of the world's best-kept secrets you need to do something to bring it to your customers' attention. Of course, whatever you do has got to be appropriate and cost-effective. Take my own situation, for example. I mostly work as a business consultant. I have thought long and hard about the right way of promoting my business. The range of options is endless – advertisements in the local and national press, public relations, brochures, flyers, exhibitions, mailshots, telesales, sponsorship, etc. Unfortunately, I don't have a bottomless financial pit, so I must get value for money. Therefore, I need to be able to measure the results.

Having considered the options I felt that most of these would not work for me because my service is not mass-market and, while most of my potential clients are likely to be within about fifty miles, I do occasionally help businesses in other parts of the UK and Europe. If I had placed an advert in the *Financial Times* (and I have tried this in a more modest way) saying 'Consultant for hire – please contact . . .' then it might cost me several hundred pounds. Hopefully I would get some calls, of which a handful would be time wasters, and I might get to see a handful of potential clients – say three. Of these, after a meeting, I might convert one and earn £1,000.

On the face of things that might look like a good payback – spend, say, £200 on an advert and get £1,000 sales back. However, sales are not profit, so you do need to take into account the full cost of achieving this one sale. Supposing the three sales visits I had to make were at all ends of the country – because that's the area the *Financial Times* covers – this might have cost me four days in preparing proposals and meetings. Now without giving away my daily charge-out rate (because I don't have a standard rate) this could have stopped me from doing £3,000 of consulting elsewhere. Suddenly, the whole advertising proposition does not look so good to me.

So what do I, and thousands of other consultants like me, do? I network in a low-cost/profile way. I keep in touch with everyone I know. I also use my contacts at business links, banks, etc. to ensure that they think of me when they have a problem client. The other thing I do is make sure my clients are always happy with what I have done for them. I am guilty of occasionally overservicing a deserving client – but I see this as an investment. This system works for me because about 90 per cent of my work comes from referrals.

But, of course, my low-cost and low-profile effort may not work for you – especially if you are a retailer, manufacturer or larger-scale service provider. What then are the options for you?

Advertising

Using local and national papers, specialist journals and magazines and TV is a way of communicating your marketing message to your potential customers. They are, of course, expensive media and are not very discriminating – you will also reach a whole lot of people you don't want. However, it is used to great effect by many businesses – look at the pages and pages of adverts that the electrical retailers bombard us with. To make advertising work for you remember the following guidelines:

- What are your objectives – what exactly is it you want to happen?
- How much are you prepared to pay to get the result you want – and don't pay a penny more than the benefit warrants?
- Make sure your message is effective in directing customer interest towards your product and your business – you may recall

amusing TV adverts that everyone remembers but cannot recall the advertiser or their product.

■ Use the right media – it may be that advertising is not right for you, just as I found out. In that case try one of the other ways of promoting your business.

If you do want to try advertising you may find these publications useful: *Willings Press Guide*, which will help you locate the right specialist newspaper or magazine, and give details of when it is published and readership numbers (this is a good general guide and it is available in most libraries); and *Benn's Media Directory*, which is a specialist subscription-only rate card used 'by the trade'. This is updated monthly so you may be able to borrow an old copy from a friend.

Leaflets, brochures and mailshots

This is probably going to be the main way that you choose to communicate with your potential customers. It is relatively cheap, simple and quick to carry out. If you have a decent computer and printer (and maybe a digital camera) you will be able to do much of it yourself. However good you are at preparing leaflets and brochures, do remember that, if you want to create impact, get professional help – even your average quick-print centre is going to be better than you at design.

Public relations

This is using the media to present your business in a favourable way without paying for the space used. Basically this is 'placing' news about your business in selected publications. These stories can be anything – new clients gained, export success, new appointments, awards, etc. The trick is writing them so that they are of wide appeal and well written so they can be used by an editor with the minimum of effort on their part. You may find that it makes sense to use a public relations consultant to help you. Why? Because they are usually ex-journalists and have all the right contacts to ensure you get into print.

Exhibitions

These are an invaluable way of sussing out competitors and their products and services – because they will be represented there. You can either exhibit or just attend. Both have their benefits. If you exhibit then you can do business (but your competitors can see you). If you do choose to exhibit but have little money see if you can share the cost with a supplier or customer or some other complementary business. A word of warning: exhibitions are very tiring, so get some colleagues to help you. Many exhibitions are by invitation only or you need to register. The exhibition organiser sells this list later so get hold of it. You may find *Exhibition Bulletin* helpful in finding what suitable exhibitions are coming up next.

Finally, at the risk of repeating myself, I must urge you to remember to evaluate whatever means of promotion you may use. This is a simple tally of enquiries, cost of media, number of customers, total sales achieved from each media activity. From these you can calculate the two key figures you want for each media activity to compare by – cost per enquiry and advertising cost per pound of sales revenue.

Place

If you are a retailer then your location is of vital importance – in fact it may be key to your success. When you are setting up a retail business or changing location consider carefully where you go. Of course, rental and buying prices reflect location. Agents talk about primary and secondary locations, which as their names imply identify their closeness to the main pedestrian traffic. If your business relies mainly on passing pedestrian traffic – if it's a gift shop, for example – then you will need to be in a primary location (but it will cost you). If, however, your business does not rely on passing pedestrian traffic (if it's a restaurant, for instance, or a cycle repair shop) then a lower-cost, secondary location (in a side street maybe) could fit the bill. In general, the factors that will decide where you locate your business are:

■ Where your customers are: Common sense dictates that you want to be as close to the largest number of customers that you can afford. Location will depend on the type of business you run and the type of access you need. Whereas a retail shop will want to be in a town or city centre, a manufacturer may find it better to be out of town in an industrial estate with good road and rail access.

■ Where your labour force is: You need to be convenient for your staff to get to, otherwise absenteeism and future recruitment may become issues. A business I know moved its offices from town to an out-of-town business park. Many of the staff now feel isolated and are considering finding new jobs.

- Availability of backup services, raw materials, etc. There may be an excellent case for locating your business in the Outer Hebrides (low cost, etc.), but, if this means everything you buy takes an extra two days to arrive and costs 20 per cent more, this might cripple your business.

- Whether you are close to competing businesses: In some instances this can be useful. Have you noticed how new- and used-car sites are situated close to each other – they act as a draw for each other. How would a close competitor affect your business?

- Image: You don't find the big firms of solicitors and accountants in run-down locations – it tends to put off their clients (and prospective clients). How does your proposed location fit your image needs?

- Cost: As with any other purchase you may make, compare costs – not just rents, but rates, service charges and setting-up costs. Also, remember that if you get it wrong you can't just walk away from a lease, which may have one to five years still to run!

Another consideration after location must be the suitability of the premises themselves. You should consider the following issues:

- Intended use: Can you use the premises you want for your business? All business properties are classified according to their approved use. For example, if you are taking over a shop previously used as a men's clothes shop you will need to apply for change of use to use it as a food shop – which you may not be given! Talk to the planning authorities and a solicitor before taking on premises.

- Size of intended premises: Are they big enough for the foreseeable future? Hopefully your business is going to grow – try to plan for this in your intended premises. Sometimes you can take additional units as you grow – but don't assume this. It may make sense to take something bigger than you need and sublet the bit you don't need (make sure you can sublet).

- Health and safety, fire regulations, etc. There is a whole raft of legislation designed to protect your staff and customers from unsafe premises and working environments. How will your proposed premises meet these? You will find the Health and Safety Commission useful for help.

- Working from home: Most small new businesses choose to work from home – it's low cost and convenient for a lot of people. Make sure you can do so. With most new houses there are prohibitions on the running of certain types of businesses from home – anything that involves noise, smell and customers visiting you. See it from your neighbours' point of view if the road is littered with your customers' cars either visiting or being repaired. Also, check out your buildings and contents insurance – your business computer may not be covered by a domestic policy.

Buy or rent: The age-old question. In most cases it makes sense to rent because you don't need to find, say, a 5 per cent or 10 per cent deposit, as you do to buy. Also you may get a twelve-month or short lease to get you going – so you are not committed for too long. Buying can be attractive only if you have a reasonable deposit, you are buying at the bottom of the property cycle and the premises you are buying are a bargain.

Channels of distribution

If your customers don't come to you then you must find some way of getting your product or service to them. I have already mentioned the cost implications of having intermediaries handle your goods before they reach the end user. Make sure that your business plan states how your distribution channel will work, why you have chosen it and what the deal is for each link. Commonly used channels of distribution are:

Retailers: Covers a multitude of specialist or general stores, which may be individually owned or part of a chain. Beware that some of them may require goods on 'sale or return', which means you take the risk if they do not sell. Others may require you to fund the stock and you may even have to pay the retailer to get your product on the shelves.

Wholesalers: The main middle person between the producer and the retailer. They buy in bulk from the producer and break it down into smaller quantities suitable for the retailer to sell to the public. Some wholesalers have become retailers by having their own outlets (cash-and-carry) and some retailers buy in such large quantities that they have become their own (and others') wholesalers – WH Smith are an example of this.

Mail order, Internet: The distinction between these two is in the way they take orders – they both supply goods in the same way. They're used to supply either specialist goods or services (Amazon, with mainly books, for instance) or a wide range (Gratton's, GUS, etc.).

Door-to-door selling, party-plan selling, telephone selling: These are all methods that rely on personal selling. Door-to-door and telephone selling are regularly used by double-glazing, conservatory and life/pension insurance companies. Party-plan selling is used for personal products such as clothes and cosmetics, and is aimed mostly at women. The selling takes place in friends' homes, with the host receiving a gift dependent on total sales made during the session.

At the end of the day whichever distribution channel you use must work for your product or service. The key things to consider are:

- Does it suit the product or service you are selling? Some products do not travel well over extended distances/time, e.g. fresh vegetables.

- Does it provide the ability to give you the sales volume you need? The Internet might provide an almost limitless sales capacity, whereas a shop may be too small to display all the stock you need to get high-volume sales.

- Is there enough profit in your product? If yours is a low-margin product then there is probably not enough money to pay for an expensive distribution channel. In general a product that is retailed is marked up by 50 per cent to 100 per cent – would this make it too expensive for the end buyer of your product or service?

- What do your competitors do? This should act as a good guide for you, especially if it seems to work for them.

I should mention in passing another way that is commonly used by manufacturers to distribute their products – especially if they are exporting (but not exclusively for this purpose). They are:

- Agents: They represent your business (and probably several others) and sell purely on commission. They secure the sale; you supply the goods directly to the end customer and secure payment. The agent then receives their commission. In some cases this may be the only way to sell your goods or services because you can't afford your own sales force – especially abroad. The downside is low agent commitment and loyalty in many cases – they frequently sell your competitors' products as well.

- Distributors: A step up from an agent in terms of commitment. They buy your product (usually in reasonable quantities) and resell it to the end user, making a margin. Distributors are only as good as you allow them to be. At their best they are fully committed, especially if you provide product training and support. Can be used to open up markets cost-effectively.

I will be covering products (the fourth P) in the next chapter when we will look more closely at product and service delivery.

Chapter summary

In this chapter we have learned how to:

- Scan the environment using PEST to identify whether any changes are happening that may affect your business and how you will minimise the effects on your business – make sure that you include this in your business plan.

- Use SWOT to review your business strengths and weaknesses and identify the opportunities and threats ahead – make sure that you include this in your business plan.

- Determine the correct marketing strategy for your business – cost leader, niche player, or just different – don't forget to outline in your business plan your strategy.

- Understand the factors that will determine the pricing of your product or service – and realise how much discounting decimates profit.

- Use promotion to get your message across in a cost-effective and measurable way – include in the business plan a summary of what you intend to do to promote your business.

- Find the right distribution channel for your product or service – don't forget to say which channel you will use in your business plan.

CHAPTER NINE

How are you going to deliver?

Chapter outline

Your customers are now lined up for you to deliver your product or service so all you have to do is make/provide it. But have you paid enough attention to this area of your business plan? What exactly do your products or services do? How do you make them or provide them? How do they compare with those of your competitors? What facilities and equipment do you need? How ready are any new products that you have in the wings? This chapter will cover the key areas of your products or services and how you make or provide them. By the end of this chapter you will have demonstrated that you can deliver your products or services on time and on price, so that they are better than your competitors.

Which parts of the business plan are covered in this chapter?

Section heading	What's covered in this section	Full business plan (external – raising money)	Full business plan (internal – performance enhancement)	Full business plan (internal – board approval)	Summary plan (external – lease, suppliers, etc.)
Products or services	Description	Yes	Yes	Yes	Yes
	Features and benefits	Yes	Yes	Yes	No
	Comparison with competitors	Yes	Yes	Yes	No
	Guarantees and warranties	Yes	Yes	Yes	No
	Patents, trademarks, etc.	Yes	Yes	Yes	No
	New products	Yes	Yes	Yes	No

Section heading	What's covered in this section	Full business plan (external – raising money)	Full business plan (internal – performance enhancement)	Full business plan (internal – board approval)	Summary plan (external – lease, suppliers, etc.)
Produc-tion or service supply	The manu-facturing process or service delivery	Yes	Yes	Yes	No
	Facilities and equipment needed	Yes	Yes	Yes	No
	Capacity planning	Yes	Yes	Yes	No
	Quality control	Yes	Yes	Yes	Yes – if it impresses
	Sources of supply	Yes	Yes	Yes	No
Comments	This section should convince the reader that you have great products or services and can deliver them.	Must be very comprehensive and not leave unanswered questions.	Must be very comprehensive and not leave unanswered questions.	This is opera-tional stuff that they will want to know.	Just tell them what you make or do and how well you do it.

What you do and how you do it

By now you should have put forward a convincing plan that shows there is a market for your product, a soundly based sales forecast and acceptable profit and cash-flow forecasts as a result. However, something rather key is missing at this stage. We need to know a bit more about your proposed products or services and how you will make or provide them. This is your chance to tell the reader of your plan what products or services you have (and about new ones on the way) and how you provide them.

Current products or services

In Chapter Three you were asked to describe what your business does as part of the business and management section. At this stage you may have mentioned your product or services in passing – now it's time to look far more closely. Your business plan must provide a detailed description and appraisal of your current and any proposed products or services.

Description

You must be able to explain to your readers exactly what service you provide or products you sell. The more precise you can be about this the better – you don't want to leave uncertainty in their mind, otherwise they will not be able to help you or will need to ask lots of questions when they meet you. If yours is a product or service that is already in common use then you will be able to describe it in a few words. On the other hand if yours is a new or innovative product or service, then you will have to be more detailed about it.

Features and benefits

As well as describing all your products and services you should list the features and benefits of each (we covered this in Chapter Seven). You may recall that a feature is a physical characteristic that does something for your customer (a benefit), which you can offer proof for. While some benefits are very concrete and measurable (faster, cheaper, etc.), others may be psychological (pride, wellbeing, status). Of course, some products or services have masses of features – look at car brochures to see pages and pages of specifications. However, if the benefit does not provide any perceivable gain to your customers it is pointless (and probably adding to the cost of the product). The following are examples of benefits that miss the mark: 'cheapness' is of no benefit to someone seeking exclusivity; 'tried and tested' is way off beam for someone wanting 'novelty'; and 'safety' may not appeal to someone wanting 'adventure'.

You could lay out the features, benefits and proof for your products or services as shown in the example below for a car:

Feature	Benefit	Proof
(1) Our car has a six-speaker stereo radio/CD player.	The quality of the sound is similar to that from most domestic hi-fi systems at a similar price.	Independent tests by car magazines have shown this.
(2) Our car has a direct-injection gas engine.	The fuel consumption is 20 per cent better than that of similar cars.	Department of Transport tests confirm this.

Feature	Benefit	Proof
(3) Our car has all-round disc brakes with antilock brakes.	The car is safer under extreme braking.	Independent braking tests at MIRA have shown this.

Comparison with competitors' products or services

To add more impact and increase the value of these benefits you should compare these with your competitors' to establish which are:

- Standard benefits – something your competitors would claim as well
- Differential benefits – something only your product or service has

It is impossible to be totally impartial when trying to compare your products with those of your competitors. The answer is to involve as many people as possible in this process. Do try to be objective and ask people to focus on the benefits – there is a temptation to get obsessed with features. Ask your customers what they think – they generally like to be asked and they will usually give you an honest assessment.

Where you can demonstrate differential benefit you have something you can exploit by bringing this to your customers' attention by such means as brochures and adverts. You may have seen the series of advertisements run by the car manufacturer Daewoo. It compared their standard features (air conditioning, free servicing, three-year warranty, etc.) and showed how these were all an extra cost on their competitors' cars. Very powerful.

Guarantees and warranties

Never underestimate the value of a warranty or guarantee in making customers buy.

- A guarantee: a formal assurance (usually in writing) that certain conditions will be fulfilled and that restitution (money back) will be made if it is not of a specified quality or standard. For instance, if you are buying a used car the garage may guarantee that the mileage shown on the odometer is correct. If the mileage is later proved to be higher than that shown, the garage will give you your money back or some other form of financial compensation.

> A warranty: a written guarantee promising to repair or replace the product if necessary within a specified period. For example, if you are buying a new TV from a shop, it will come with a standard twelve months' warranty that promises that it will be repaired free of charge (parts and labour) during that period if it breaks down. A replacement product may be offered free of charge if it cannot be economically repaired.

You should state what guarantees or warranties your product or services have and how these compare with your competitors'. In many cases a guarantee or a warranty has no significant cost because your product or service is so good (never goes wrong), the cost of remedying the problem is so little or the product is low-value and treated almost as disposable. A good warranty can help sell a product or service and enhance its perceived benefit.

Something special

Is there something special about your product or service that you want to take full commercial advantage of? There are various ways of doing this, some of which offer some degree of legal protection to stop your ideas being ripped off.

> Proprietary position. There may be something quite unique about your product or service that cannot be legally protected (or you may not want to). For example, have you a special skill that enables you to do a job that your competitors can't?
>
> Patent. This protects how something works and offers twenty years' protection for an invention. Basically, you tell the state how you made your unique invention and in return it will give you the means to prevent anyone else subsequently using your idea. Works in UK, USA and Europe, but many East European states, China and Third World countries ignore patents. For further help contact the Patent Office.
>
> Trademarks protect what something is called. These can be a word, a logo, a symbol, a picture and so forth by which your product is identified with you. It must be distinctive and applies only to tangible goods (excludes services). For further help contact the Trade Marks Registry.
>
> Design registration protects how something looks. This enables you to register a shape, design or new decorative features of a commercial product. Protection applies to industrial articles destined for large-scale production and lasts for 25 years. For further help contact the Design Registry.

> Copyright protects work on paper, film or record. This gives
> protection against the unlicensed copying of artistic and creative
> works such as books, films and songs. Protection lasts for seventy
> years after the death of the copyright holder, or fifty years after
> publication if later. For further help contact the Stationers' Hall.

In all the above you will have to demonstrate originality and that
what you are trying to protect does not bear too close a similarity to
another protected item.

New products and services

So far we have looked at products or services and have made an
assumption that they are ready for the marketplace. Of course, it may
well be that you are about to launch a new product or service.

Case study

Barry Powell was planning to launch a new product for the
Christmas market. His business plan showed a significant sales
forecast during Year 1. He believed that it would take six months
from the initial design through to production and delivery to customers.

Design started in April with the intention of having it ready for
production in October – plenty of time to scale up production for
the Christmas market. The design was completed on time but
trouble started at the prototype stage. They just could not get it to
work – despite the use of outside consultants and the best brains
from a nearby university. After many late nights and all but a
rethink of the original design the prototype was ready – two
months late. A small production facility was set up, but, try as they
might, the reject rate for early products was unacceptably high – it
was eating away all the profits and reducing volumes of output.
Eventually, two months later than planned, acceptable products
were available. Unfortunately, the slippage of four months meant
that they missed the Christmas market altogether and the product
was shelved – by the next year it was anticipated that it would have
been old hat.

I asked Barry what advice he would give anyone in a similar situation. His advice was quite simple. Be pessimistic about time
scales. If you really think it will take six months from start to fin-

ish, plan on its taking twice as long – twelve months. If you take this approach you will not go far wrong.

You must state the readiness of all your products for the marketplace. I must stress that, if you are in the process of preparing new products and services for launch, it always takes longer than planned and anticipated. The reader of your plan will not necessarily share your optimism about how quickly you can get it ready. The real killer in terms of credibility is where you have included sales revenues (and profits) in Year 1 of your business plan for a new product or service that even by your own admission 'is not quite ready yet'. If the success of your business is dependent on this, please be ultra-cautious in terms of its launch date.

The process of developing new products and services is basically the same for all and should include:

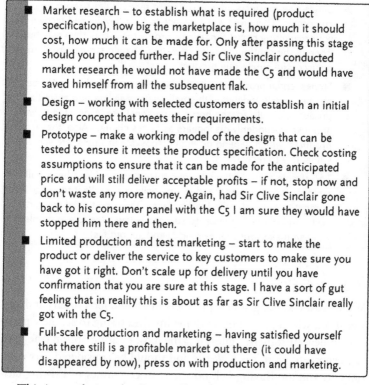

- Market research – to establish what is required (product specification), how big the marketplace is, how much it should cost, how much it can be made for. Only after passing this stage should you proceed further. Had Sir Clive Sinclair conducted market research he would not have made the C5 and would have saved himself from all the subsequent flak.

- Design – working with selected customers to establish an initial design concept that meets their requirements.

- Prototype – make a working model of the design that can be tested to ensure it meets the product specification. Check costing assumptions to ensure that it can be made for the anticipated price and will still deliver acceptable profits – if not, stop now and don't waste any more money. Again, had Sir Clive Sinclair gone back to his consumer panel with the C5 I am sure they would have stopped him there and then.

- Limited production and test marketing – start to make the product or deliver the service to key customers to make sure you have got it right. Don't scale up for delivery until you have confirmation that you are sure at this stage. I have a sort of gut feeling that in reality this is about as far as Sir Clive Sinclair really got with the C5.

- Full-scale production and marketing – having satisfied yourself that there still is a profitable market out there (it could have disappeared by now), press on with production and marketing.

This is not designed to be an all-inclusive checklist for product or service development but it is the minimum that you should be stating in your business plan. For each of your new products you should state:

- What stages have been fully completed
- What stages have yet to be completed with an estimate of time and resources (people, equipment, money, etc.) needed to complete

Before we leave the subject of new products and what makes a winner, here are a few thoughts.

- **Single products:** always very risky but frequently the starting point for most inventors or businesspeople. A single-product business is very vulnerable to competitors, changing fashions, etc. Make sure that you quickly establish a family of related products to broaden your product range, thereby reducing the risk.
- **Single-sale products:** ideally you want repeat sales to your customers. This gives you a chance to build loyalty and recover all your marketing costs. Single-sale products have all the costs but none of the continuing sales revenues. I would struggle to think of a successful single-sale product.
- **Nonessential products:** over the last twenty years the high street has become inundated with small retailers selling non-essential products, usually for the home or personal use. A new fad arrives and just as suddenly disappears as tastes change. Also, these products, which depend on high disposable incomes, are very vulnerable to recessions.
- **Too simple a product:** while your customer may like a beautifully simple product or service, this simplicity may make it too easy for competitors to enter the marketplace – they don't need technical skills, and marketing effort to succeed is low. One to avoid unless you can make your money quickly and get out fast.

Diversification

While we are looking at new products we should look briefly at diversification, which at its most extreme involves trying to sell new products to new customers. I guess it is the most exciting option (the grass is greener, etc.) but it is *high-risk* and should be considered very carefully, as you are leaving behind the twin certainties of existing customers and existing products.

If you are considering launching new products or services then the sensible option is to market them to your existing customer base. A further point to note is that, if you are considering a higher-risk diversification strategy, the profit margins must be correspondingly higher. The diagram below puts it all neatly into perspective.

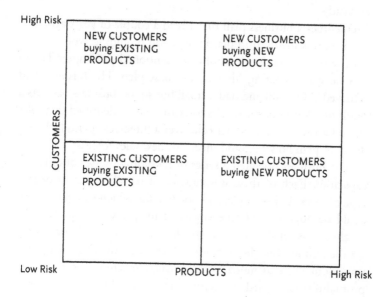

Using this matrix gives a clear sense of the risk and if it helps you in deciding on your strategy for product and customer development it will have been worthwhile. Boring though it may be, the safest and frequently the best strategy is to sell more of the same or similar products to your existing customers. Maybe the best plan for new-product development is the one adopted by most of the mainstream car manufacturers – facelifts and improved value for money. This is what kept the Ford Escort at the top for over twenty years – gradual improvement without significantly changing its customer base.

The manufacturing process or service provision

Anyone looking at your business plan is going to ask the question, 'How do you do what you do and how are you going to produce/deliver this increased sales volume that your business plan is showing?' Well, do you have a convincing plan? This is not an area to ignore because if yours is a growth business then, as sure as eggs is eggs, you will run out of capacity at some stage.

Case study

I remember a business plan that I read a couple of years ago. The business was involved in plastic injection moulding (you remember my friend Ken Lewis whom we mentioned in Chapter Three) and he was preparing his new business plan. His business had achieved ISO 9000 and had a small but sound business base. As a result of his very detailed sales forecast he had identified that sales should grow by some 40 per cent over a three-year period. We sat down to plan how he could meet this new sales forecast.

The business operated a series of moulding presses of different capacities. Each of these was capable of handling only a certain type of work. For example, a plastic box lid, which was quite large, could be done on only the largest of his presses. However, that machine was capable of doing smaller work, such as plastic cutlery for the airlines. But the cost of production on the largest machine was about twice as much as the smallest machine. To maximise profitability he needed to carefully plan his production so that jobs were run on the lowest-cost presses.

The maximum profit was made when he could have a press working on one job for several days. This minimised downtime, as tool changes between jobs and initial test batches cost time and money. At the same time another consideration was his supply of raw materials. Being quite tight on cash, he needed to minimise stocks of raw materials. Ben, who was responsible for production scheduling and stock ordering, placed daily/weekly orders to ensure just the right amount was available.

Perhaps now you can appreciate the apparent complexity of his business. The prospect of 40 per cent more business, while good news, posed a real planning headache. However, Ken knew his business, so together we simulated how his business might handle this extra work. We worked out how much work each machine could handle on 8-, 12- and 24-hour shifts with no job changes. This gave a maximum theoretical capacity – but it did not at this stage allow for breakdowns, tool changes and essential maintenance. However it did tell us that his existing presses could comfortably handle the additional work in the next two years but by Year 3 it was getting tight.

We then did a more accurate production plan that took into account tool changes, maintenance and a downtime allowance for breakdowns. On the basis of this a crude production plan emerged for Years 1 to 3. This showed a combination of 12- and some 24-hour shifts in Year 1, increasing to more 24-hour shifts in Year 2 and almost entirely 24-hour shifts by Year 3. This process flagged up three issues that needed to be addressed:

- **New press** – by Year 3 one of his older presses would need to be replaced to improve efficiency and hence capacity. This needed financing (cash flow) and installing, which would reduce capacity for nearly a week. These had to be shown in his business plan.

- **Space** – extra business meant extra space was needed for increasing quantities of raw materials and customers' stock waiting to leave. It was anticipated that in about twelve months' time they would be stuffed to bursting point – this would clog up production. How could extra space be provided? There was not a spare unit nearby but there were others available on that industrial estate. Another option was to store offsite in locked containers. Both were costed and evaluated. In the end the plan was to rent another unit nearby and move finished stock into it – this was shown in the business plan.

- **People** – additional production and supervisory staff were needed in each of the years. The problem was that it was almost impossible to get good people. They had tried employment agencies, temp agencies, etc. – none had been very satisfactory. How could they recruit the extra people they needed? Suddenly a brainwave arrived. Ken asked his existing staff if they had any ideas. They did the bulk of the recruitment for him by asking friends (and a few relatives) if they wanted to join them. Over the months they increased the workforce in a low-cost way.

All these issues were identified right from the onset and included in Ken's new business plan. This saved him from nasty surprises later. Make sure your business plan addresses all these issues.

How do you do it?

Of course the exact detail will vary according to whether you are in retailing, manufacturing or service provision – but there will be many similarities between them, and certainly the approach must be the same.

This is perhaps the most complicated operation of all – so you will need to explain to your reader how you make your product or deliver your service. Remember, they are not technical, so keep it at a simple level. Here are some of the key things to mention.

Do you make or buy?

Do you make the product or supply the service yourself, or do you buy it in? It is possible that you buy in part of the product (sub-assemblies) and assemble and test it to arrive at your end product, which carries your name.

Case study

Phil Goymour, who ran TSS, used this approach. He had tried full-scale manufacture of all his products but found that it was not necessarily the most cost-effective way of doing things. He also discovered that some of the parts he needed were difficult to source and very expensive for him to buy because he used only a handful each year. He looked closely at his business and recognised that its strengths were in designing and servicing his products – not making them. Consequently, he decided that he would buy in subassemblies from a handful of carefully selected quality suppliers. Believe it or not, this was cheaper and quicker, and resulted in a better product being delivered. If you provide a service do you subcontract it out? You must explain how you do things and why.

Describe the process

You will need to prepare a description of the manufacturing or service delivery process. You will need to tell your reader how you make your product or deliver your service now and any changes you may be going to make over the course of the business-plan period. Of course, your challenge is to make your complicated process understandable to your non-technical reader. As an aside at this stage I will warn you that, if you are trying to secure venture-capital funding, they will have a technical expert who will read your business plan – and they will know their onions. They will spot any weaknesses in your story!

I suggest that, if you are trying to satisfy these two different readers, you include a summary of your manufacturing process within this section of the business plan and a more technical write-up in the appendices. Be ready for questions such as, 'How does your manufacturing process compare to that of your competitors?' If this is an important consideration, include a comparison in your business plan.

Plant and equipment

What are the key items you have or will need for your business to meet the required sales forecasts? A brief description will suffice and an explanation of what it does within your manufacturing process or service delivery. You must also state what capacity each major piece of plant or equipment has. This will let your reader know how much spare capacity (if any) you have and how easily you could gear up for increased sales (over and above those forecasted).

You should state what shift pattern you work (e.g. seven days/twenty-four hours) and what capacity you can achieve at each. If your plan needs new plant and equipment, show how this will be integrated with existing – installation, pre-testing, etc. Make sure that what you say here ties up with what your funding section says that you are going to do.

Technical expertise

If you run complicated equipment, what do you do if it breaks down or needs setting up? Do you have in-house engineering expertise? Are your operators properly trained to use their equipment?

Do you have personnel who are conversant with health-and-safety legislation, fire regulations, first aid, etc?

Quality systems

How do you control and monitor the quality of your product or service? Are your processes documented, up to date, and followed religiously? Is there a 'care' culture or a 'don't care' culture?

If you have some quality systems, have you considered obtaining

ISO 9000 to reinforce them (contact the British Standards Institute to find out more).

You may be interested to know that your customers may force you to adopt recognised quality standards. If you want to be a supplier to, say, Ford, you would need to comply with their assurance system. This would apply even if you were not supplying materials to go into their vehicles!

Stock-holding policy

Unless you make to order, you will need to keep stocks of finished goods to ensure that in peak times of demand your customers don't have to wait too long. What is your policy – do you guarantee supply within a specified time? If so what stock do you need to hold to meet this commitment?

Sources of supply

Poor suppliers can cripple a business. More and more businesses are relying on 'just-in-time' processes, which can mean that when something goes wrong stocks immediately dry up. How vulnerable is your business to supplier failure? Your business plan should explain what bought-in materials and services you require. The key things to look at and include in your business plan are:

- Key materials and services. What are the key items that you buy in? Do you have to buy minimum quantities? And how many weeks' worth of production is that? Can you buy these items from more than one supplier? Do you have back-up suppliers? What would happen if you could not get one or more of these key items? Do you have substitute products or services you can use? Are all your materials and services readily available, or do they sometimes become limited in supply?

- Relationship with suppliers. What sort of relationships do you have with your suppliers? Are they good relationships, or does paying your suppliers late at times put a strain on things? What are their credit terms? Do you have any contractual relationship with them – guaranteed scheduled deliveries based on a production schedule, for instance?

- Choice of suppliers. How did you choose your key suppliers? Was this based on price, quality and reliability? How good are they? Do they have recognised standards, for instance? Do you have back-up suppliers in case your main supplier goes bust or fails to deliver on time?

Chapter summary

In this chapter we have learned that:

- There is a difference between features (useful) and benefits (essential) in products and services – your business plan must show how yours excel over those of your competitors.

- If there is something special and unique about your product or service you can legally protect it from being ripped off by your competitors – if you have any patents, trade marks, etc., include them in your business plan.

- You need to be realistic about the state of readiness of any new product or services you may have – make sure that your business plan gives these details.

- Diversification is very high-risk and not always the best option.

- You need to be fully conversant with your production process or service delivery system – and be able to explain it in your business plan.

- Suppliers are important to your success – your plan should state how you select and deal with them.

CHAPTER TEN

What about the people?

Without people your business is powerless. How do you grow without having the people to handle this extra business? You can't. Your business plan must demonstrate that you have quantified what human resources you will need over the period of your business plan. It must also show how you will recruit these in a timely manner and retain them within your business. Finally, your business plan must explain what systems you have in place to ensure that you can manage these resources successfully. This chapter will cover the key areas: developing a human resources (HR) plan; recruiting and retaining staff, and the essential ingredients of an HR system. By the end of this chapter you should have reviewed your HR processes and set out a convincing HR strategy within your business plan.

Which parts of the business plan are covered in this chapter?

Section heading	What's covered in this section	Full business plan (external – raising money)	Full business plan (internal – performance enhancement)	Full business plan (internal – board approval)	Summary plan (external – lease, suppliers, etc.)
People	People requirement, including recruitment and retention	Yes	Yes	Just people-requirement information	No
	Insurance	Yes	Yes	No	No

Section heading	What's covered in this section	Full business plan (external – raising money)	Full business plan (internal – performance enhancement)	Full business plan (internal – board approval)	Summary plan (external – lease, suppliers, etc.)
Comments	This section should convince the reader that you recognise the importance of people within your business.	Must be very comprehensive and not leave unanswered questions.	Must be very comprehensive and not leave unanswered questions.	Just tell them how many people you need and when – usually central recruitment and retention.	Tell them nothing – this is none of their concern, unless they ask.

People are important

You will recall that in Chapter Three I was stressing the importance of people within a business. Some years ago, when running a programme for owner-managers at Warwick University, I used to 'grant' the delegates any one wish for their businesses. An interesting discussion usually followed. The businesses would have a wish list that usually comprised:

- More good customers
- More money
- More good people

When pressed to narrow it down to just one wish, they would rationalise it as follows:

- More good customers: They felt pretty confident that their businesses would grow and that they had good products which they could sell. While it would be nice to 'magic up' some more customers today they believed that through their own efforts they would get them anyway. They would therefore pass on the offer of more customers.

- More money: Certainly only a handful of the businesses were cash rich and most of them could use more cash. Overall they felt that while their businesses were profitable and growing they would be supported by their banks if they needed more finance. Perhaps a friendly word in their bank manager's ear would be nice but no more than that at this stage.

- More good people: It was at this point that there would be a consensus among all the delegates – regardless of the health of

> their businesses. Those who had growth businesses were always trying to recruit additional staff. They universally found it frustrating and frequently complained that they could not find good people and struggled to keep those that they already had. On balance they agreed that they would accept the help of the magic wand to solve this problem.

It is universally agreed that people are the most important asset in any business, so your business plan should include a section that explains:

- How your human resource (people) systems works
- What your human resource requirements are
- How you will recruit new staff
- How you will retain existing staff

People systems

The key to keeping people is to manage them properly. I have seen well-paid people leave jobs because the business did not seem to be interested in them: they were poorly managed; achievements were not recognised; and they really could not see their value to the business. In their own words, they felt it was time to go. Your business plan must show how you cover the following:

Human resource manager

It seems strange that we recognise such things as finance, production and sales as important enough to warrant at least a manager and in bigger companies usually a director, yet neglect the discipline of human-resource management. I can understand that if yours is a small business you can't afford a full-time HR manager – you probably don't need one. However, regardless of the size of your business, there is still an HR function to be fulfilled.

At least have someone nominated as being responsible for the HR function even if it is alongside their other responsibilities. Having done that, give them some training, because employing people is a potential legal minefield for the uninitiated. The Institute of Personnel Management is a useful point of contact and Croner's sell a range of employment guides (with updates) aimed specifically at SMEs. The success of your HR function depends on this person.

Staff handbook

You may think this is just for big companies but many of my clients employing as few as fifteen employees have found this document worthwhile. Get an employment solicitor to put it together for you – it is almost available 'off the shelf' but an expert will ensure it exactly meets your requirements.

Don't confuse this with a contract of employment (which follows). The staff handbook tells employees 'how things work' within their company. It will include such things as engagement, promotion and transfer; general discipline; disciplinary procedure; grievance procedure; performance appraisal; how and when salaries are paid; holiday arrangements; time off; sickness entitlement; statutory sick pay; maternity leave and pay; company pension scheme; equal-opportunities statement; personal records; data protection; health and safety; security; company property; private mail and telephone calls; inventions and patents, conflicts of interests; confidential matters; copyright; company vehicles.

Contracts of employment

This is a must for any employee who has been with you for longer than two months and works more than sixteen hours per week. If you do not provide a written contract then an oral contract may be held to apply or statute will construct one – best to be safe and make sure you give everyone a written contract as soon as possible.

It will contain the basic employment details relevant to that person. For the contract to be valid it must be signed by the employee and returned to the company – each party keeps a copy. It contains: rate of pay; payment intervals; hours of work; holidays; place of work; job title; sick pay; pension arrangements; notice period; status of contract – temporary or permanent; union representation. You will notice some areas of slight overlap with the staff handbook.

Job descriptions

Not required by law but a sensible idea. This is a written statement of what the employee's main roles and responsibilities are, whom they report to, etc. Its importance goes further than that – it's a symbol of your business's professionalism. It recognises that you have thought carefully about why they are employed and the role within the business.

As an aside, when you are looking to recruit, one of the first things applicants ask for is a job description for the job on offer – if you don't have one you will never attract the best people because they expect one.

Appraisal systems

Not required by law but more than just a sensible idea. This is a process (usually six-monthly or annual) whereby each employee is formally reviewed by their direct manager. The outcome should be an assessment of: what they have done well; what they have done badly; where they go from here (which may include further training, promotion, etc.) When done well, this is a superb tool for motivating and retaining employees.

Unfortunately, in most cases it is done badly and so can demotivate employees. The key is in the preparation by both sides and honesty. The end result is an agreed action plan, which is designed to maximise the involvement and performance of the employee. Often linked to merit pay reviews.

Structure and delegation

Unless you are a one-person business there is a need to manage people. Show how your businesses is structured (an organisation chart will help). Show the line of command for supervisors or managers for the key areas of the business, such as accounts, administration, production, sales, HR, etc. This will help highlight if any of them have too many people directly reporting to them.

A business cannot grow unless it develops. This usually involves delegating power to capable subordinates. In the UK there is a point at which most businesses stop growing, which is around thirty employees. These businesses have the potential to grow but the person at the top is unable to delegate and does not build up a management structure to handle growth. Had this happened, more businesses would grow to achieve far greater financial success. Your business plan should show how your business will be structured for growth.

Pay rates

Show how you set pay rates. Do you regularly review them against those of your competitors?

Explain any system of staff grades with rates of pay for each. When were they last reviewed and increased?

Training

Show the formal systems you have in place to assess and address training needs. Have you considered Investors in People (IiP) as a means of matching training to company objectives?

You can find out more about IiP from your local Chamber of Commerce or Business Link.

Key employees

Do you have back-up if any key staff are sick or leave suddenly? State how you would cope if someone were on jury duty for three weeks. Are your processes written down so that anyone can follow them?

Personnel records, PAYE, NI

Are your records up to date – especially PAYE and NI? Have you got written copies of P45s, P60s, P11Ds, and any disciplinary actions?

Termination and redundancy

Hopefully, you will not need to let people go because their job has disappeared. It is, however, probable that as your business grows or changes some of the original employees will no longer be suitable – this is normal. It will be necessary to negotiate an exit route for them.

You must be familiar with employment law – what is fair and reasonable. Get it wrong and you may end up before an industrial tribunal. This is where following procedures in your staff handbook will help. In the case of redundancy you should speak to both an employment solicitor and ACAS.

People requirements

If your business is growing or changing do you know what extra or different people you will need for each part of your business? You should have an HR plan that shows how many extra people you will need for production, sales, administration, finance, etc., if your turnover is going to grow as planned. When do you need them? Don't forget that it takes time to recruit and train? Your HR plan should show all your requirements:

- Number of new people needed
- When they are needed
- Job skills they will need
- Anticipated remuneration costs
- Additional resources needed (equipment, workspace, cars, etc.)
- Any redundancies (if reducing parts of the business) – timing and costs

This list will enable you to prepare a recruitment programme.

Plan to phase recruitment. It is easier to successfully bring in ten people over six months than try to do it all in one month – assuming your business plans can accommodate this approach. The main purpose of the HR plan is to let you handle change in a planned and organised way, which will be easier to handle than doing it in a blind panic.

Recruitment

How do you recruit to meet your HR plan? There are a range of options that you can use; each has its own advantages and disadvantages:

- Recruitment agency: Takes pressure off you to do the bulk of the legwork (placing advert, interviewing, assessing applicants, etc.). Of course all this service has a real cost, which may be beyond your budget.

- Do your own recruitment: Can be low-cost if you can draft simple adverts and have time to sift through the replies and perform interviews. If you have an HR manager, this is their job – if not, it's yours. You will need to know how to interview because if you are not experienced you will make a real mess of it.

- Using tests to measure people: We are all different but we conform to certain characteristics and types. Obviously, if you can identify these at the interview stage you can increase your chances of getting the right people for the jobs you need filling. Also, within a business you need a mix of all types, a bit like a football team, where you need a mix of forwards, midfielders, backs and a goalkeeper. In your business you need a similar mix to ensure that, as a team, you can work together. Your business plan should state what you can do to improve your recruitment process.

- Finding employees: Regardless of whom you use to do the recruiting you have got to find the employees. An agency may know where to look, but do you? It is possible that you are going to need specialist staff who will be difficult to find. If this is the case your chances of successfully recruiting them are lower and it will take longer – make sure you take this into account in your recruitment plan.

■ Induction programme: You must state how your induction programme works. You should have a written-down procedure that guides the new employee into the organisation and into their job. It should include skills training (if required). You should not have a policy of 'sink or swim' – you have invested too much in getting the new employee to do this.

Your business plan should show all of the above. This is your evidence that you are a business that is professional and capable of managing the HR growth process.

Keeping your people

Having got a settled workforce what do you do to keep them?

Case study

I remember talking some years ago with the owner-manager of a business that designed and made a fairly hi-tech product. They employed about thirty employees in bright, modern, air-conditioned offices. As I walked round I got a real feeling that this was a great place to work – people seemed to be buzzing. I stopped and asked a few of the staff about how the place was managed and what they liked. I can't remember everything they told me but these were some of the main ones. On a Friday they had a dress-down day. The staff who usually had to wear suits said that this was great because it hardly felt like being at work. Others liked it because for one day a week it made everyone look the same, be they bosses or production staff – no us and them. Another thing they liked was the fact that on Friday they also had a 'wind-down' session in which for a couple of hours in the afternoon they could just chat. Everyone attended this session – even the salespeople who were out of the office got back in time. What was so special about this session? I asked. I was told that it was a chance for everyone to talk about what had happened to them that week – share experiences. They even talked about business issues and solved a few problems.

It was clear to me that Friday obviously set them up nicely for the weekend, but what else was good about working there?

Communications. It seemed that everyone knew what was going on in the business – there was a minimum of secrets. There was an open-door policy – anyone could talk to the boss. There was a profit-share system that people understood and each month a 'scoreboard' was put up indicating how the profit-share pool was progressing. The overall feeling I had was that people worked hard and enjoyed being there. How did I know they worked hard? I saw the accounts for the business – very nice!

Whatever you do to create a good working environment you must continue with it – no one-day wonders that you don't continue with. Also, they must be cost effective. I once worked for a company in Glasgow where we operated a nine-day fortnight. Each week one half of each department had the day off – yes, a long weekend every other week. It was brilliant. No, the company was not being generous: it made sure we worked our full 47½ hours each week. This was done by earlier starts, shorter lunches and going home later at night. It all worked out really well because it helped us miss the worst of the traffic. In fact, it was a win-win situation for both the company and the employees. Of course, this may not work for your business.

Your business plan should state what you do to retain staff. It must be more than just words such as, 'We aim to keep all key members of staff . . .' There must be some substance. The following are recognised ways of retaining staff:

- Remuneration package: Provide an overall package that is recognised as being the best in the area or as good as the business can afford. The package includes basic salary, performance-related bonuses, holiday entitlement, free medical cover, free life assurance, company mobile phone, company car, free petrol, subsidised meals, subsidised accommodation, employee share option schemes, etc. Mention in your business plan what they get, and don't forget to allow this full cost in your financial forecasts. Overall, a full package could add in the region of 20 per cent – 50 per cent extra to base salary costs.

- Promotion opportunities: Ambitious employees change jobs on a regular basis – every two years is not uncommon. They do it for two main reasons: career progression and remuneration. If you have already looked after the money aspect (see above) then you need to give them an opportunity to progress within the company. Ideally your business should have a structure that enables this. Does your business plan show how you can enable good staff to stay? Have you already mapped out a promotion route for your key staff? Sometimes it may not be possible to promote because the business is too small. However, you can change someone's role by giving them additional responsibilities (at a higher level) and passing some of their lower-level responsibilities on to someone else.

■ Training and personal development: The next most important element after remuneration and career progression is development. If you can develop your staff – pay and provide time for them to study for a qualification that will help them and the business – you are both winners. Usually it is common practice to make the employee receiving this benefit agree to stay for a period after qualification – say twelve months. I have known companies pay for their employees to attend leisure-interest programmes that are unrelated to work. State in your plan what development plans you have for your staff.

■ Creating a great working environment: Informal days (such as the idea we saw earlier), company days that allow you all to get out of the business to have a leisure day, calling each other by first names, getting rid of offices, working in teams – these all help to make work better. What do you do?

■ Communications: Too many businesses operate on the 'mushroom' principle on their employees: keep them in the dark and then dump on them from a great height. If something is wrong in the business people soon find out. There is no sense in trying to pretend it never happened. If you have just lost a major customer then people should be told as soon as possible to stop them picking up misleading information on the grapevine. An old boss of mine used to have a 'fireside' chat. He would come out into the general office and talk to everyone about the 'state of the nation'. This way he got a good feeling for how we felt about things. Others use newsletters, email, etc. What do you do to communicate? And how?

■ Good management: Finally, the best way to keep people is to manage them properly. I have worked in businesses where I knew I was underpaid and there were no immediate prospects for progression. Why did I stay? My boss was brilliant – understanding, supportive, encouraging, found out what made me tick and talked about my interests. He knew how to manage me. Your plan should include management training for senior managers.

Insurance – protecting your business

An important part of protecting your business is making sure you take out the right insurance cover. Insurance is an area often overlooked by most new businesses and a lot of more established businesses. Your business plan must show that you have considered your insurance requirements and taken out appropriate cover. Insurance cover falls into two categories. There is insurance you must have by law:

- Employers' liability – covers you as an employer if one of your employees is injured or ill as a result of working for you (and you have been negligent).
- Motor insurance – if you drive a car it needs to be insured for business use.
- Engineering equipment – some equipment (pressure vessels and lifting tackle) must be inspected and certified as safe annually; you can combine insurance and maintenance in one policy.

And there is insurance you may want:

- Buildings and contents insurance – a must because it covers any loss to these from fire, flood, theft, etc. If working from home, do check your policy to see if business use is covered.
- Loss of profits insurance – worth getting because it covers your business if it is disrupted by fire (or some other insured peril). This means that you can pay wages, rent and so forth while your business is unable to trade.
- Loss of money insurance – worth getting if your business carries a lot of cash.
- Goods in transit insurance – worth getting if your business delivers physical products to customers that could be damaged or lost.
- Public liability and product liability – covers your liability to the public if they are injured on your premises (public liability) and any injury or damage to their property that happens as a result of the use of your product (product liability). Worth getting if the court judgements in the USA are anything to go by.
- Professional indemnity – almost essential if you are a business consultant and give advice. This covers you if your client suffers any loss as a direct result of your advice. You will need this to get on to most consultants' registers.

Keyman insurance – pays your business if one of your key employees dies. The cash enables you to replace them – either temporarily or permanently.

It is difficult to envisage all the situations that may be worthwhile insuring against. Do talk to a broker to obtain advice.

Chapter summary

In this chapter we have learned that:

- Having good HR systems really does help you to get the best out of your employees and make sure you are fully protected against unfair legal action – make sure your business plan shows what systems you have and how they work.

- Your business will need new people and new skills as it grows and changes. Your business plan needs to show that you have taken this into account and planned your HR requirements.

- Getting new people is a difficult process – you can't just phone up a shop and order them. Your plan needs to demonstrate how you will recruit new people.

- Having recruited good people, how do you keep them? It's not just a matter of cash: it's the whole thing. Your plan needs to show what you have in place to keep your key people.

- Don't forget to insure against the common business risks and legal necessities – your business plan should show you are adequately covered.

CHAPTER ELEVEN

Making it all happen

Chapter outline

You may think that you are finished with your business plan – you are not. Certainly you may have written a plan that looks good to you on paper but three big issues remain: telling everyone about the plan, delivering the plan, and controlling the business. Telling everyone about the plan is down to you. You must do it in a way that is sensible for your business and fits with your style. How you are going to do this does not need to be in your business plan – but be prepared if they ask you the question. You must include in your business plan how you intend to deliver the plan and control the business. This chapter will cover the key areas: communicating the plan, action plans and business controls. By the end of this chapter you should have set out your action plans and business controls within your business plan.

Which parts of the business plan are covered in this chapter?

Section heading	What's covered in this section	Full business plan (external – raising money)	Full business plan (internal – performance enhancement)	Full business plan (internal – board approval)	Summary plan (external – lease, suppliers, etc.)
Business controls	Financial systems	Yes	Yes	No	No
	Other systems	Yes	Yes	No	No
	Action plans	Yes	Yes	Possibly – ask.	No

Section heading	What's covered in this section	Full business plan (external – raising money)	Full business plan (internal – performance enhancement)	Full business plan (internal – board approval)	Summary plan (external – lease, suppliers, etc.)
Comments	This section should convince the reader that you will deliver and control the business.	Must be very comprehensive and not leave unanswered questions.	Must be very comprehensive and not leave unanswered questions.	They know this already but they may want the action plans.	Tell them nothing – this is none of their concern, unless they ask.

Communicating your plan

Your business plan has achieved its first objective – secured the money, got board approval, clinched the lease, etc. So now what do you do? You have got to deliver against your business plan because there are a lot of people out there with high expectations – new investors, the bank, new landlord, staff and so forth. If you did not involve your managers in the preparation of your business plan then your plans may come as a bit of a surprise to them. Almost certainly they will not know the detail of the business plan. Further down the line there will be staff who are blissfully ignorant of your plans and what may be expected of them. You have to get them all on board so that they are all rowing together – and in the right direction. Depending on the size of your business, then, the communication process could be as my friend Tim Holmes does.

Case study

Tim Holmes employs about 25 people in his marketing communications business. His senior management team comprises five people. Each year when Tim produces his business plan he follows a tried and tested process. He involves all his senior managers. Tim sets the overall objectives and communicates these to the team. They then work on a plan that can deliver against these.

A sales forecast is prepared – not by Tim, but by his new business manager and operations manager. The accountant prepares a cost budget and a series of profit and loss forecasts (with sensitivity analysis). Eventually a full business plan is prepared with the involvement of the senior managers.

So what about the other twenty employees? How do they find out about the business plan? They have a conference offsite, where

Tim and his senior management team present the new business plan to them. They spend a day together – play silly games, have fun – and by the end of the day everyone knows what is expected of them. Any changes of strategy are explained. If there are to be any new work practices then separate workshops are organised during work time to explain these. Action plans are drawn up, responsibilities assigned and follow-up monitoring meetings held.

This process of involving and communicating the business plan works for Tim – but what do you do? There are basically two ways of communicating your business plan:

1 Company meeting: You gather the whole business unit – which could be the whole company or just a division, factory, department – and present the plan to everyone. Bearing in mind the mixed nature of the meeting (tea person through to managers) do not present in detail but use a broad brush. After the main meeting use your subordinate managers to hold team meetings to explain the next level of detail.

2 Cascading meetings: You gather your senior managers and introduce the plan to them. Because of the nature of the meeting the discussion will be in some detail. The senior managers will then be responsible for holding separate meetings with supervisors and staff to explain the plan to them. Depending on how large your business is there may be several levels of meeting.

You should use whichever approach is appropriate to your size of business and your personal style. The end result should be the same – everyone in the business knows in appropriate detail what the plan is.

Delivering the plan

Communicating the plan is all well and good but how do you ensure that action happens? You must make people responsible for delivering parts of the plan that are appropriate to them. You will remember that in Chapter Three we looked at missions, objectives, tasks and action plans under hierarchy of goals. The diagram opposite may help put this all into perspective:

Business Planning Process		Action Plans & Feedback Systems		
Missions and Objectives	Tasks	Action Plans	A C T I O N S	R E S U L T S

The tasks, as you will remember, are the high-level activities that need to be achieved to meet the objectives, e.g. we may need to work with our customers to improve communications and scheduling. Creating them is the last part of the business planning process. The use of them is the starting point of the action planning process. The detailed action plans follow on from this and show the low-level activities that need to be carried out to fulfil the tasks, e.g. what we do on Monday morning. However, this is a two-way process:

1   Starting with the key tasks, set out action plans that assign responsibilities to named individuals with dates by which these actions must be completed. If a key task leads to several action plans for different individuals that follow on from each other, then each individual should have their own action plan and have a copy of those that immediately precede and follow theirs. That way they can be aware of what needs to be done before their tasks and whom they will holding up if they don't achieve them on time.

2   Using the action plans, individuals will perform their actions, which should lead to the detailed results expected. Ongoing review should be carried out to make sure that the desired results actually happen. This can be done by means of review meeting with the individual's supervisor/manager. If results are not keeping up with the action plan, additional resources or time may be made available to ensure the key tasks are achieved. The least desirable option is to revise the action plan, as this will mean changing the key tasks, which will have an impact on the business objectives.

You will need to make sure that your business plan leads on to action plans that deliver the business objectives. This section should state that action plans have been issued and a summary of these should be included here. However, the detailed action plans should be included within the appendices.

Business controls

Nobody is going to give you money without being convinced that you will use it properly. You may have prepared a winning business plan but the proof of the pudding (as they say) is in the eating (or in your case the delivery). Your business plan must show what systems you have in place to monitor and control your progress. These will include a whole range of business controls.

Financial controls

Budgets

Regardless of whether you are a limited company, partnership, sole trader or whatever, you need to know where you are and how this compares with where you want to be. From your detailed financial projection should come a budget for the next twelve months. This is a key tool for monitoring your actual financial performance. My suggestion would be that you take your profit and loss forecast from Chapter Five and use this as a monitoring tool by showing each month's actual results and variance against budget. The example below shows the current month position (Month 3) and the year to date position (which in this case is the sum of all the three months so far this year).

Beechwood Enterprises: profit-and-loss forecast, year ended 31 May 2001

	Month 3			Year to date		
	Budget	Actual	Variance	Budget	Actual	Variance
Sales income	20,000	15,000	−5,000	80,000	70,000	−10,000
Less cost of sales	10,000	11,000	1,000	40,000	50,000	10,000
Gross profit	10,000	4,000	−6,000	40,000	20,000	−20,000

	Month 3			Year to date		
	Budget	Actual	Variance	Budget	Actual	Variance
Expenses:						
Rent	1,000	1,000		3,000	3,000	
Salaries	10,000	9,000	−1,000	30,000	27,000	−3,000
Heat and light	1,000	900	−100	3,000	2,700	−300
Stationery	500	600	100	1,500	1,700	200
Total expenses	12,500	11,500	−1,000	37,500	34,400	−3,100
Net profit before tax	−2,500	−7,500	−5,000	2,500	−14,400	−16,900
Tax						
Net profit after tax	−2,500	−7,500	−5,000	2,500	−14,400	−16,900

In this example we can see that:

1 Sales are below budget for both Month 3 and for the year to date.
2 Cost of sales is above budget for both Month 3 and for the year to date.
3 Stationery is above budget for both Month 3 and for the year to date.

The actual versus budget comparison has revealed these three variances, which now need to be investigated to find out why they happened and what can and will be done to stop them from happening again.

Fortunately, there has been a favourable variance: heat and light is below budget. Also, since there are nine months left to run before the year end, there is time to stop the rot.

The key figures you will need to know (and how frequently you will need to use this) are:

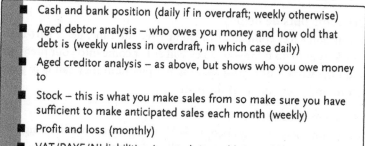

- Cash and bank position (daily if in overdraft; weekly otherwise)
- Aged debtor analysis – who owes you money and how old that debt is (weekly unless in overdraft, in which case daily)
- Aged creditor analysis – as above, but shows who you owe money to
- Stock – this is what you make sales from so make sure you have sufficient to make anticipated sales each month (weekly)
- Profit and loss (monthly)
- VAT/PAYE/NI liabilities (quarterly/monthly/monthly)

- Balance sheet (at least quarterly but ideally monthly)
- Key operating figures: break-even, key costs, sales, etc. (monthly)

Key ratios

Don't forget that when you prepared your business plan you worked out a series of key ratios. You can now use these to control and monitor the day-to-day performance of the business. For example, if your key ratios stated that debtor days were going to be, say, 45 days and actual days are running at 55 days, what does that tell you about the business? Things are getting worse and you are taking longer to collect your money. So what's the answer? Start to look at the whole process from invoicing through to the money ending up in your bank account. There are a whole host of reasons why this may happen – isolate the problem and act.

Accounting system

Of course to know where you are financially you will need some system to provide these figures. What you will need, of course, depends on: the size of your business, your legal status (limited company, sole trader, etc.), volume of transactions, complexity of business, VAT-registered, etc. Here are some of the options:

Be self-sufficient
If yours is a simple business and you have some basic accounting skills then do it yourself – but only if you have time. Don't let 'doing the books' be an excuse for your business not to be successful. There is a whole range of preprinted accounts book systems available from all the main stationers. A word of warning – they work but they are quite complex (despite their claims). If you are computer-literate and a reasonable user of spreadsheets then use this approach – it is infinitely flexible and you know how it works.

Get some outside help
If you don't feel competent or don't have the time, get a part-time bookkeeper to do it for you. They will either come into your premises to do the work – or if your space is at a premium they can take your records away and do it off the premises.

Your own accountant
If your business employs people, is VAT-registered and has a significant number of customers and suppliers, it may be time to have your

own full-time accountant. They can do most of the administration, wages, debt chasing and so forth, as well as the bookkeeping. They do not need to be qualified – experience will be enough for most small businesses. If, however, you are raising venture capital they will want you to have a qualified accountant (but not necessarily). Of course, if the volume of transactions is high – and only you will know when this is; it's when the accountant runs out of time each month end – then a computerised accounting system could be the answer.

Computerised accounting systems

The beauty of a good computerised accounting system is that you can process information more quickly, automate some activities (e.g. invoicing, statements, aged debtor reports, etc.), and produce a large variety of reports at the click of a button. If you use the mainstream accounting packages, your external accountant/auditor can take a data disk from you and complete the annual accounts offsite.

Computerised accounting packages cost from £20 to £100,000 – depending on complexity and the number of users you require to have access. Remember to budget to have training, otherwise you will not get any benefit from the new package. A final warning: if you use an accounting package do remember the accounting principles I mentioned in Chapter Five (accruals, prepayments, stock adjustments, etc.), otherwise, when you run the financial reports, they will be garbage.

Other controls

Sales control systems

If you have a sales force it will need controlling – and it becomes more difficult the greater the size. The overriding objective must be to deliver what the business needs and not what the salesperson likes doing. Your business plan will have established an overall sales forecast. If you have more than one salesperson then this will need splitting up in some equitable way – if only to stop them treading on each other's toes and visiting the same customers. This splitting up can be geographical (north, south, east, west, for instance), by product or service category or by some other customer allocation method (premium customer, standard customer). The overriding rule is: *salespeo-*

ple need to be managed, otherwise they will tend to suit themselves rather than the company.

As a minimum level of control all salespeople should submit contact reports (either daily or weekly) and weekly or monthly sales reports. The contact report is (as its name implies) purely a report on a sales meeting (client name, date, location) and what occurred at that meeting. The sales report should be used to generate sales statistics so that reasons for success (or lack of it) may be identified.

For example, a new sales report could show the following:

Weekly New Sales Activity Report				
Date	No of Phonecalls made	No of Quotations sent	Appointments	£ Sales
				Conversion Rate
Totals				

From this type of report you could establish weekly activity levels and conversion rates. This could be used to monitor sales activity and direct resources to increase sales.

Marketing control systems

Just as you would seek to monitor and control sales activity you should also monitor your marketing spend. This may take the form of using the monthly budget figure (from your financial forecasts) and quantifying what return you have received in terms of column inches of public relations (PR); responses to advertisements (by publication), etc.

Other control systems

These would, of course, vary according to whether you make a product, sell a service or retail goods. However, they could include:

■ Manufacturing – for each machine you may record hours worked, good stock made, rejects, etc.

- Personnel – for each employee you could log sickness, unexplained absences, etc. as a percentage of hours/days worked and follow up those with higher than average figures. The follow-up could include return-to-work interviews, etc.
- Quality – you could record returned goods as a percentage of sales made and compare with the acceptable standard. Variances would prompt investigation to ascertain why.

The Balanced Business Scorecard

You will have noticed that most of the control systems outlined so far have a strong financial bent. What would supplement them nicely would be a more holistic system that took account of the following:

- Vision
- Mission
- Strategy
- Critical success factors
- Performance measures

The Balanced Business Scorecard does this by recognising all the stakeholders in a business and any strategic objectives you may have for them:

- Shareholders (measured primarily by financial measures)
- Customers (measured primarily by marketing measures)
- Internal business (measured primarily by operational measures)
- Growth (measured primarily by innovation/learning measures)

The balance of these is shown in the diagram below:

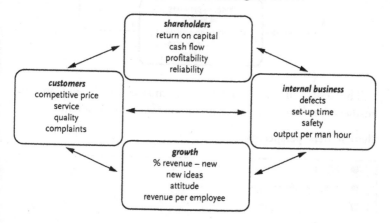

Of course, all these interests are not in conflict: they are in balance to achieve the business objectives. In fact, they must all be achieved to ensure the overall business success. Now if you add to this framework some typical measures that you might use, you can see a new business control system emerging:

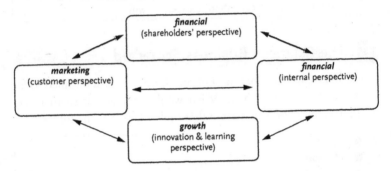

And finally you can see how the whole business planning and control feedback system works in the diagram below:

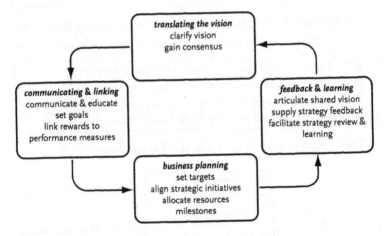

The actual choice of measure you choose will depend on your business, but here are some that you may want to consider:

Shareholders' perspective

- ROCE
- gross profit margin
- net profit margin

- overheads
- break-even point
- cash in hand
- bank position/relationship
- debtors
- creditors
- reliability

Customer perspective

- enquiries
- proposals sent/accepted
- contracts started/finished
- contract size/duration
- new work
- repeat business
- customer satisfaction
- ABC analysis
- cohesion
- image change

Internal perspective

- labour
- overtime
- resource utilisation
- work in progress
- rejects
- maintenance
- sales/employee
- (capacity) utilisation rate
- complaints
- queues

Growth perspective

- technology leadership
- manufacturing learning

- product focus
- time to market
- internal business performance improvement
- workforce empowerment
- service innovation
- continuous improvement
- partnerships
- patent applications

Your business plan must inspire confidence that you will control the business (especially if it has now got someone else's money). You do this by stating what control systems you have in place to show you are on the ball.

Chapter summary

In this chapter we have learned that:

- The business plan may start in your head and end up in a document – but how are you going to ensure that everyone in the business is familiar with it?
- If you are going to achieve the success you have planned you need to get people responsible. We call these action plans and they should be in your business plan.
- To make both you and your investors/bankers feel more comfortable about your business you must control it. What systems do you have in place to make sure things don't go wrong – or if they do you spot them quickly so you can correct them? Are these in your business plan?

CHAPTER TWELVE

A final thought

Your business plan checklist

By now you are heaving a sigh of relief and preparing to have your masterpiece – the business plan – neatly bound and sent out in the post. However, human nature being what it is, there is an even chance that you have forgotten something, so here I am to remind you of a few things. The checklist below should save you from the worst of your mistakes and omissions:

	Action	Tick off when done
1 **Content of plan** ■ Check that you have completed all the sections ■ Check that all the numbers are consistent in executive summary and forecasts ■ Check that your plan has been reviewed by others ■ Check that your plan has passed the reality test ■ Check that all your appendices are included	Compare your business plan to section headings in Chapter 2.	

	Action	Tick off when done
2 Style ■ Check that it looks professional – headings, bullet points, spelling, etc. ■ Check that all the numbers add up ■ Check that sections written by different people are consistent with rest of plan	Let someone else read the plan – maybe your secretary.	
3 Sending out plan ■ Check that accompanying letter is personalised and professional ■ Make sure that letter, plan and appendices go out together ■ Send out in good time before meeting	If you've got a secretary, let them do the lot – that's what they are really good at. Otherwise it's up to you to send it all out.	
4 Preparing for the meeting ■ Make sure that all the presentation team are thoroughly familiar with all the plan ■ Practise your presentation in front of someone and get feedback ■ Get all your visual aids ready and looking professional	Practice makes perfect.	
5 The big day ■ Phone up the day before to make sure meeting is still as planned ■ Make travel arrangements the day before ■ Travel together and aim to allow plenty of time to arrive five minutes early ■ Wear appropriate businesslike clothing	Make sure you all meet up and travel together on the day.	

	Action	Tick off when done
■ At the meeting stick to your presentation plan ■ Allow time for questions ■ Listen to what your audience has to say ■ Good luck		
6 **After the big day** ■ Phone up after agreed time to ascertain outcome if it has not been communicated to you		

Your next business plan

I know that this seems like a strange thing to be saying – just after you have prepared your current business plan. However, business plans are not for ever – they do have a 'sell-by date'. Certainly within a year you will need to be preparing your next business plan update, if only because you have completed the first year of your business plan. In a way this will be a case of: stop, check to see if your business plan is still valid and roll it on another year. This will involve making your old Year 2 the next-year budget. This may mean some additional detailed work to prepare budgets and action plans. You may at the same time want to redo the final year of your business plan – to give the full three- or five-year view.

Of course, it is possible that for one reason or another your business is way off course. Sales and profits may be well below forecast. In that case your original plan may not be valid and a fresh plan is required that takes account of the current factors. Even if sales and profits are above those forecast in the plan, you should still review the plan. It may be possible that a more ambitious plan can be prepared and achieved.

Hopefully this book has helped you to success with this business plan – in which case it will have been the best-laid business plan for you. Good luck. Enjoy your success. And here's to the next one.

Appendices

Financial projection sheets

Profit and loss forecast – twelve months
Profit and loss forecast – quarterly
Profit and loss forecast – five-year summary
Cash flow forecast – twelve months
Cash flow forecast – quarterly
Balance sheet forecast – quarterly
Balance sheet forecast – five-year summary
Break-even analysis – five-year summary
Key performance ratios – five-year summary
Budget sheet – monthly and year to date

These spreadsheets are available from the author's website:
www.paulbarrow.co.uk

Business name:

Profit and loss forecast – twelve months   Year ended: (20XX)

	Month 1	Month 2	Month 3	Month 4	Month 5	Month 6	Month 7	Month 8	Month 9	Month 10	Month 11	Month 12	Total for Year
Sales income													
Less cost of sales													
Gross profit													
Expenses:													
Total expenses													
Net profit before tax													
Tax													
Net profit after tax													
Cumulative net profit after tax													

Business name:

Profit and loss forecast – quarterly

	Year ended: (20XX)				Total for Year	Year ended: (20XX)				Total for Year
	Qtr 1	Qtr 2	Qtr 3	Qtr 4		Qtr 1	Qtr 2	Qtr 3	Qtr 4	
Sales income										
Less cost of sales										
Gross profit										
Expenses:										
Total expenses										
Net profit before tax										
Tax										
Net profit after tax										
Cumulative net profit after tax										

Business name:

Profit and loss forecast – five-year summary

	Year 1 (20XX)	Year 2 (20XX)	Year 3 (20XX)	Year 4 (20XX)	Year 5 (20XX)
Sales income					
Less cost of sales					
Gross profit					
Expenses:					
Total expenses					
Net profit before tax					
Tax					
Net profit after tax					

Business name: _____

Cash flow forecast – twelve months

Year ended: (20XX)

	Month 1	Month 2	Month 3	Month 4	Month 5	Month 6	Month 7	Month 8	Month 9	Month 10	Month 11	Month 12
Inflow:												
Total inflow												
Outflow:												
Total outflow												
Monthly movement												
Opening bank balance												
Closing bank balance												

Business name:

Cash flow forecast – quarterly

	Year ended:	(20XX)				Year ended:	(20XX)		
	Qtr 1	Qtr 2	Qtr 3	Qtr 4		Qtr 1	Qtr 2	Qtr 3	Qtr 4
Inflow:									
Total inflow									
Outflow:									
Total outflow									
Monthly movement									
Opening bank balance									
Closing bank balance									

Business name: **Balance sheet forecast – quarterly**

	Opening Balances	Qtr 1 (20XX)	Qtr 2 (20XX)	Qtr 3 (20XX)	Qtr 4 (20XX)
Fixed assets					
Cost					
Accum. depreciation					
Net book value					
Current assets					
Stock and WIP					
Debtors					
Prepayments					
Bank and cash					
Current liabilities					
Trade creditors					
Accruals					
Bank overdraft					
Short-term loans					
Net current assets					
Net assets					
Financed by					
Share capital					
Reserves					
Long-term loans					
Capital employed					

Business name: Balance sheet forecast – five-year summary

	Opening Balances	Year 1 (20XX)	Year 2 (20XX)	Year 3 (20XX)	Year 4 (20XX)	Year 5 (20XX)
Fixed assets						
Cost						
Accum. depreciation						
Net book value						
Current assets						
Stock and WIP						
Debtors						
Prepayments						
Bank and cash						
Current liabilities						
Trade creditors						
Accruals						
Bank overdraft						
Short-term loans						
Net current assets						
Net assets						
Financed by						
Share capital						
Reserves						
Long-term loans						
Capital employed						

Business name:	Break-even analysis – five-year summary				
	Year 1 (20XX)	Year 2 (20XX)	Year 3 (20XX)	Year 4 (20XX)	Year 5 (20XX)
Total revenue					
<u>Direct costs</u>					
Materials	____	____	____	____	____
Direct labour	____	____	____	____	____
Total direct costs	____	____	____	____	____
Gross margin	____	____	____	____	____
Gross margin %	____	____	____	____	____
<u>Fixed costs</u>					
____	____	____	____	____	____
____	____	____	____	____	____
____	____	____	____	____	____
____	____	____	____	____	____
____	____	____	____	____	____
____	____	____	____	____	____
____	____	____	____	____	____
____	____	____	____	____	____
____	____	____	____	____	____
____	____	____	____	____	____
____	____	____	____	____	____
____	____	____	____	____	____
	____	____	____	____	____
Total fixed costs	____	____	____	____	____
Break-even point (BEP)	____	____	____	____	____
Margin of safety	____	____	____	____	____
Target profit	____	____	____	____	____
Total fixed costs	____	____	____	____	____
Break-even profit point (BEPP)	____	____	____	____	____

Business name:

Key performance ratios – five-year summary

	Year 1 (20XX)	Year 2 (20XX)	Year 3 (20XX)	Year 4 (20XX)	Year 5 (20XX)
Growth:					
Sales growth percentage (%)	____	____	____	____	____
Profitability:					
Return on capital employed (%)	____	____	____	____	____
Risk/solvency:					
Gearing (%)	____	____	____	____	____
Interest cover (Times)	____	____	____	____	____
Trading performance:					
Gross profit percentage (%)	____	____	____	____	____
Net profit after tax percentage (%)	____	____	____	____	____
Working capital:					
Current ratio	___ :1	___ :1	___ :1	___ :1	___ :1
Quick ratio	___ :1	___ :1	___ :1	___ :1	___ :1
Debtor days (Days)	____	____	____	____	____
Stock turn days (Days)	____	____	____	____	____
Fixed asset use:					
£ sales per £ of fixed assets	£ ____	£ ____	£ ____	£ ____	£ ____

Business name: **Budget sheet – monthly and year to date**
                                    Year ended: **(20XX)**

	Month x			Year to date		
	Budget	Actual	Variance	Budget	Actual	Variance
Sales income						
Less cost of sales						
Gross profit						
Expenses:						
Rent						
Salaries						
Heat and light						
Stationery						
_____						
_____						
_____						
_____						
_____						
_____						
_____						
_____						
_____						
_____						
_____						
_____						
Total expenses						
Net profit before tax						
Tax						
Net profit after tax						

Sources of help

General help

The British Chambers of Commerce
Manning House, 22 Carlisle Place, London SW1P 1JA
Tel: 020 7565 2000
Email: info@britishchambers.org.uk
Website: www.britishchambers.org.uk

British Standards Institution
389 Chiswick High Road, London W4 4AL
Tel: 020 8996 9000

Business Link Helpline (to find out how to contact your nearest
business link)
Tel: 08457 567765
Website: www.businesslink.co.uk

Companies Registration Office
Crown Way, Maindy, Cardiff CF4 3UZ
Tel: 029 20388588

HM Customs and Excise
Thomas Paine House, Angel Square, Torrens Street, London
EC1V 1TA
Tel: 020 7865 3100; fax: 020 7865 3171
Website: www.hmce.gov.uk

Health and Safety Executive
Rose Court, 2 Southwark Bridge, London SE1 9HS
Tel: 020 7717 6000

Board of Inland Revenue
Somerset House, Strand, London WC2R 1LB
Tel: 020 7667 4000

Department of Social Security
Press Office, Richmond House, 79 Whitehall, London SW1A 2NS
Tel: 020 7238 0800; fax: 020 7238 0763
Website: www.dss.gov.uk

Department of Trade and Industry
1 Victoria Street, London SW1H 0ET
Tel: 020 7215 5000 or 6024

How to find professional advisers

Institute of Chartered Accountants in England and Wales
PO Box 433, Chartered Accountants Hall, Moorgate Place,
London EC2P 2BJ
Tel: 020 7920 8100

Institute of Chartered Accountants in Scotland
27 Queen Street, Edinburgh EH2 1LA
Tel: 0131 2255673

Institute of Chartered Accountants in Northern Ireland
Belfast BT1 5JE
Tel: 028 9032 1600

Law Society
113 Chancery Lane, London WC2A 1PL
Tel: 020 7242 1222

Banks, finance, insurance

British Bankers' Association
Pinners Hall, 105–108 Old Broad Street, London EC2N 1EX
Tel: 020 7216 8800; fax: 020 7216 8920
Website: www.bba.org.uk

Association of British Insurers
51 Gresham St, London EC2V 7HQ
Tel: 020 7600 3333; fax: 020 7696 8999

BVCA British Venture Capital Association
Essex House, 12–13 Essex Street, London WC2R 3AA
Tel: 020 7240 3846; fax: 020 7240 3849
Email: bvca@bvca.co.uk; website: www.bvca.co.uk

DTI Loan Guarantee Scheme
Small Business Service
1 Victoria Street, London SW1H 0ET
Tel: 020 7215 5363; fax: 020 7215 2773

Marketing

Acorn
Published by CACI Market Analysis
CACI House, Kensington Village, Avonmore Road, London
W14 8TS
Tel: 020 7602 6000

Annual Abstract of Statistics
Published by the Office for National Statistics
1 Drummond Gate, London SW1V 2QQ
General enquiries: 020 7233 9233
Website: www.statistics.gov.uk

Aslib (the Association for Information Management)
(can provide list of specialist business libraries in UK)
Staple Hall, Stone House Court, London EC3A 7PB
Tel: 020 7903 0000; fax: 020 7903 0011
Website: www.aslib.co.uk

Benn's Media Directory
Miller Freeman PLC
Sovereign Way, Tonbridge, Kent TN9 1RW
Tel: 01732 364 422

Business Monitor series
The Stationery Office
51 Nine Elms Lane, Vauxhall, London SW8 5DR
Tel: 020 7873 0011

Exhibition Bulletin
London Bureau
272 Kirkdale, Sydenham, London SE26 4RZ
Tel: 020 8778 2288

Guide to Official Statistics
Published by the Stationery Office
Central Office, Great George Street, London SW1P 3AQ
Tel: 020 7270 6363

Hollis Press & Public Relations Annual
Harlequin House, 7 High Street, Teddington, Middlesex TW11 8EL
Tel: 020 8977 7711

ICC Information Ltd
Field House, 72 Oldfield Road, Hampton, Middlesex TW12 2HQ
Tel: 020 8481 8720

Key Note Ltd
Field House, 72 Oldfield Road, Hampton, Middlesex TW12 2HQ
Tel: 020 8783 0755

Key British Enterprises
Dun and Bradstreet Ltd
Holmers Farm Way, High Wycombe, Bucks HP12 4UL
Tel: 01494 4222000

Kelly's Business Directory
Kelly's Directories
Windsor Court, East Grinstead House, East Grinstead, West Sussex
RH19 1XB

Kompass
Windsor Court, East Grinstead House, East Grinstead, West Sussex
RH19 1XA
Tel: 01342 335819; fax: 01342 335745
E-mail: jmason@reedinfo.co.uk; website: www.kompass.com

The Market Research Society
15 Northburgh Street, London EC1V 0AH
Tel: 020 7490 4911

Market & Opinion Research International (MORI)
32 Old Queen Street, London SW1H 9HP
Tel: 020 7222 0232

NOP Market Research Group Ltd
245 Blackfriars Road, London SE1 9UL
Tel: 020 7890 9000

The Retail Directory
Newman Books
32 Vauxhall Bridge Road, London SW1V 2SS
Tel: 020 7973 6402

Protecting your good ideas

The Chartered Institute of Patent Agents
Staple Inn Buildings, High Holborn, London WC1V 7PZ
Tel: 020 7405 9450; fax: 020 7430 0471

Patent Office/Design Registry/Trade Marks Registry
Cardiff Road, Newport, Gwent NP9 1RH
Tel: 01633 814000; fax: 01633 813600
Website: www.patent.gov.uk

The Worshipful Company of Stationers & Newspaper Makers
Stationers' Hall, Ave Maria Lane, Ludgate Hill, London
EC4M 7DD
Tel: 020 7248 2934

People

ACAS
Advisory, Conciliation and Arbitration Service
ACAS Reader Ltd, PO Box 16, Earl Shilton, Leicester LE9 8ZZ
Tel: 01455 852225

Croner, CCH Group Ltd
145 London Road, Kingston upon Thames, Surrey KT2 6SR
Tel: 020 8547 3333; fax: 020 8547 2638
Email: info@croner.cch.co.uk; website: www.croner.co.uk

Chartered Institute of Personnel and Development
CIPD House, Camp Road, London SW19 4UX
Tel: 020 8971 9000; fax: 020 8263 3333
Website: www.cipd.co.uk

Federation of Recruitment and Employment Services
36–38 Mortimer Street, London W1N 7RB
Tel: 020 7323 4300

Tolley Publishing Company Ltd
Tolley House, 2 Addiscombe Road, Croydon, Surrey CR9 5ZX
Telephone 020 8686 9141; fax: 020 8686 3155

Index